I just read this book, and now I want to go talk with my kids about sex. And here's the best part—I'm actually looking forward to it, not dreading it. Jessica and Joel talk about hard topics in such an easy way, I'm ready to do the same. This book crushes any notion that talking about sex and talking about Jesus don't mix. Jessica and Joel are honest about sex and also persistent about looking at the Savior—a rare combination that parents and kids need today.

Jack Klumpenhower
author of *Show Them Jesus: Teaching the Gospel to Kids*

Nobody wants to talk to their kids about sex. When it comes to the big conversations, we often need a field guide to help us navigate the trenches with our kids. In this fun little guidebook, Joel and Jessica give parents the tools to talk about sex in a manner that is productive, useful, and immensely scriptural. Using sound gospel-oriented reasoning, good judgment, personal stories, and helpful conversational tools, *Mom, Dad...What's Sex?* helps parents to have conversations about sex with their teenage children without slipping into legalism. After reading this helpful book, parents will go from feeling trepidation regarding "the big talk" to feeling ready and empowered to help their children navigate these confusing times in a manner consistent with the gospel of Christ. In addition, Jessica Thompson and Joel Fitzpatrick are just fun people, and their personalities shine though in this book. *Mom, Dad...What's Sex?* is a must-have for the shelf and nightstand of parents everywhere.

Scott L. Keith
executive director, 1517 the Legacy Project

Like so many, I never had a conversation about sex with my parents, and in the church, sex was spoken of negatively—that we should abstain from it, or we would be condemned by it. Now that I have two children of my own who are growing up in an increasingly confusing sexual world, I'm so grateful for this book. It gives us a solid foundation of the gospel in relation to sex, and it provides practical guidance on starting the conversation with our children. Jessica and Joel remind us our ultimate help comes from the Holy Spirit, but they also show us how we can better navigate the awkward but necessary talks we need to have with our kids.

Grace P. Cho
writer and managing editor of *The Mudroom* and *Grace Table*

Mom, Dad...What's Sex? is everything we need to navigate the conversations we might have been avoiding. With a clear understanding of the powerful influence of our culture, Joel and Jessica provide us with gospel-centered guidelines for having open and ongoing dialogue with our kids about sex and sexuality. Your kids may be living in shame because of their sexual sin, or they may be living in pride because of their purity. Or maybe your kids are on the cusp (which is probably younger than you think) of needing to begin "the talks." Regardless of where you are in your parenting journey, this book will be a lifeline for you. I can't recommend it highly enough.

Jeannie Cunnion
author of *Mom Set Free*

A lot of "sex talks" focus on what not to do. While affirming moral absolutes, Jessica and Joel are convinced that the gospel fills us and our children with a larger story of redemption that includes our sexuality. This is a great book to read together with the whole family.

Michael Horton
professor, Westminster Seminary
author of *Core Christianity*

Mom, Dad...What's Sex? provides families with a clear vision, a winsome apologetic for the Bible's sexual ethic, and practical guidance—everything from social media to porn to same-sex attraction, y'all! But to just say that would miss the point. Joel and Jessica's goal is to celebrate Christ, who enters the hot mess of our sexual brokenness and brings redemption. Get this book and let it guide your family conversations.

Jared Kennedy
pastor of families, Sojourn Community Church
author of *The Beginner's Gospel Story Bible*

Finally—a gospel-saturated book for parents that provides important insight and instruction on how to effectively engage a child's heart on the subject of sexuality. It also offers healing for parents who are still waiting for *their* parents to have "the talk" and who had to figure things out on their own. In *Mom, Dad...What's Sex?*, Jessica Thompson and Joel Fitzpatrick take parents on a bold journey to discover God's beautiful design for sex and provide much-needed gospel-based perspective and practical advice on how to effectively combat culture's "if it feels good, do it" narrative. This book needs to be read and reread in every home!

Traylor Lovvorn
speaker, podcaster, and executive director of *Undone Redone*

Mom, Dad... What's Sex?

JESSICA THOMPSON
AND JOEL FITZPATRICK

HARVEST HOUSE PUBLISHERS
EUGENE, OREGON

Cover design by Bryce Williamson

Cover photos © ljubaphoto, SKrow / iStockphoto

Published in association with the literary agency of Wolgemuth & Associates. Inc.

This book contains stories in which people's names and some details of their situations have been changed to protect their privacy.

Mom, Dad...What's Sex?
Copyright © 2018 by Jessica Thompson and Joel Fitzpatrick
Published by Harvest House Publishers
Eugene, Oregon 97408
www.harvesthousepublishers.com

ISBN 978-0-7369-7266-6 (pbk.)
ISBN 978-0-7369-7267-3 (eBook)

Printed in the United States of America

18 19 20 21 22 23 24 25 26 / BP-SK/ 10 9 8 7 6 5 4 3 2 1

To every single one of my friends and family members who had to endure awkward conversations about sex during the writing of this book. Thank you. Your input helped craft what you hold in your hands.

JESSICA

To my beautiful bride, Ruth—thank you for encouraging and supporting me. Your love and care were instrumental in the writing of this book.

JOEL

Contents

Part 3: How to Have Great Conversations About Sex

Why We Need the Bible's Story About Sex

A Foreword by
Justin S. Holcomb and Lindsey A. Holcomb

Awkward.

That's how most parents describe talking to their children about sex. Ask your friends how their parents told them about sex, and if their parents didn't avoid it completely, you will likely hear hilarious stories of parents stammering, blushing, and sweating.

It is awkward because sex is private and personal. It is awkward because many parents feel guilt for sexual sins they committed or shame and suffering because of sexual sins committed against them.

But there is another way to describe talking to your child about sex—loving.

It is loving because it is desperately needed. Children today are exposed to sexual language, images, and behavior before they are developmentally prepared to handle them. It is inevitable that your children will be shaped and influenced about sex. However, the culture does not have to be the dominant force in shaping your children, and your children do not have to "conform to the pattern of this world" regarding sex. You are more powerful than you might imagine. Parents can be the primary influencers of their children's emotional, spiritual, and psychological development regarding sex.

Parents who share age-appropriate information about sex can counter unhealthy social norms regarding sexuality and relationships. Children are constantly learning social norms from peers and media. Our job is to teach them what is expected or appropriate regarding sex and relationships.

Not to talk to our children about sex as they grow up in a hypersexual culture is like launching them, with no preparation, into a "Choose Your Own Adventure" story that unlikely to have a happy ending. This isn't a guilt trip for parents, but a reminder of how much our children need us to communicate, influence, answer questions, and listen when it comes to sex.

Talking to our children about sex is loving not only because it is needed but also because it is a marvelous opportunity to teach them about themselves, God, and the world God made.

Answering questions with age-appropriate and candid responses will build confidence and trust with our children. Regardless of their age, our children will have lots of questions about their bodies, other people's bodies, desires, and life in general. Talking about sex also invites explanation about why God created the gift of sex, how powerful sex can be for love or harm, and the important role sex plays in God's plan for creation.

Mom, Dad...What's Sex? is a gift from Jessica and Joel to parents. They write about hope and grace and how the unconditional love of God informs our conversations with our children about sex. It encourages us to be honest and candid as well as humble, loving, patient, and hopeful.

This book is packed with wisdom that comes from experience. Jessica is the mother of three children, and she is known for her distinctively grace-filled books and talks on parenting. *Mom, Dad...What's Sex?* is not abstract or theoretical but comes from life with three children. Joel is the father of two children and an ordained minister in the

Presbyterian Church in America. Jessica and Joel are also brother and sister. Their extended family shares a wonderful sense of humor, they love to laugh, and they do not take themselves too seriously. You'll be able to see all this in this book.

When talking about sex, content is important, but so is tone. Our children need the tone of *Mom, Dad...What's Sex?* rather than a hyper-sexualized free-for-all from our culture or rants on avoidance from sexually repressed fundamentalists.

Christians too often express a so-called Puritanical view of sex in which sex is dirty and an abasement of human morality. However, God made humans inherently sexual beings, both in their biological nature as male and female and in their desires for physical intimacy in the context of marriage.

According to Stanley Grenz, "the assertion that sexuality belongs to the essential nature of the human person arises from two Christian doctrines, creation and resurrection. God created us as embodied beings, and in the resurrection recreates us in like fashion. Together the two doctrines confirm a basically holistic anthropology that includes our sexuality."[1]

In the Bible, human sexuality begins in the garden of Eden, where God created all things good, including the male and female and their sexuality, and commanded humans to "be fruitful and multiply" (Genesis 1:28). Sex was God's idea and an expression of shalom, peace, love, and unity.

After this original goodness, sin entered the world, all good things were distorted, and everything went haywire, including sex. About God, sex, creation, and sin, Robert Gagnon writes, "Scripture regards the urge to gratify intensely pleasurable sexual desires as part of God's good creation. Nevertheless, given their often-insatiable quality, Scripture also recognizes a constant threat to the Creator's norms."[2]

Thus, from the biblical perspective, there is one conclusion. The proper context for sex is the "permanent, monogamous relationship called marriage. This perspective is the basic teaching of the Bible in both Old and New Testaments."[3] At the same time, there is much more in the Bible regarding sex, shalom, sin, grace, and hope.

The Bible makes clear that the pattern for sex was created by God but that it was frequently violated—and these violations are repeated throughout human history. God does not leave things broken, however, and is always at work healing the sin, wounds, and brokenness related to in human sexuality. God redeems and restores. He reestablishes the original peace and goodness that was violated by the Fall. God's re-creation is not simply a repair job so things work a bit better than before. Rather, in his creative and loving power, God finds a way to restore his creation in such a way that everything is even better than it was before sin mucked everything up.

We pray that power will be released in your family through this book and you will begin a legacy of sexual wholeness that will last for generations.

Introduction

My eyes began to water under the harsh glare of the fluorescent lights. Or was I (Jessica) holding back tears because of the question my nine-year-old had just asked me? There we were, walking through Walmart, when I heard the most timid of voices ask, "Can you please tell me about sex?"

I tried to wiggle my way out of the bind. "We already read that book. Remember? Do you need to know more than that right now?"

"Mom, please tell me everything."

The dreaded phrase. I wasn't expecting it so soon. Nine seems too young. Nine seems innocent. And for goodness' sake, in Walmart of all places!

Despite these hesitations, I knew I needed to seize the moment. The two of us were hardly ever alone. I needed to take the time. So there, with the Rollback smiley face staring at us with that huge grin as though it knew what just happened, I started in on the conversation. I started with how it was meant to be. I started where the Bible started. One man, one woman, naked and unashamed.

My nine-year-old, however, wasn't so interested in the story of Adam and Eve, and so she pressed. How does it happen? What goes where?

So as we picked out the cheapest toilet paper and grabbed cleaning supplies, we had *the talk*.

The situation was less than ideal, and I wondered if I was doing things the right way. Shouldn't we be sitting down? Shouldn't she be older? Shouldn't we have a Bible and some other authoritative book with stick figures? I second-guessed everything I said. Somehow we made it through the store and through the conversation. Being in public made *the talk* less awkward and more awkward at the same time. My daughter had good questions, really good ones, which went into more than just the how of sex. Those questions led us back to the Bible, to the truth of our brokenness, to the hope of redemption. God's goodness and mercy followed us up and down every aisle of that store.

I have confidence in God's ability to take my frail efforts, my stumbling words, my inadequate knowledge and use them to help my daughter see how amazing and powerful he is. That confidence in his ability to use my words gave me hope, and I return to it when I think about how my daughter's understanding of sex will develop.

> I have confidence in God's ability to take my frail efforts, my stumbling words, my inadequate knowledge and use them to help my daughter see how amazing and powerful he is.

I told my baby that she could ask me anything at any time, and she has. Since that conversation we have had many follow-up talks. My hope has never been in my ability to communicate everything exactly right. Rather, it will always be in my God—who uses all things for our good and his glory—and in his glorious gospel, which transforms even awkward, stilted conversations into moments where grace shines through.

Afraid to Talk

My experience and feelings about talking with my daughter about sex aren't abnormal. Most Christians are afraid to talk with their kids about sex. We are afraid that talking about sex will stir up desire that was not there before. We wonder, *Am I saying too much?* but we're also nervous that saying too little will incite curiosity that leads to conversations with their friends or to Google searches. And we are afraid that when we set clear boundaries for kids, they will be incited to break these boundaries.

We desire to see our kids grow up without the shame and burden of exposure to sex or sexual activity too early in life. And we speak in the context of our own sexual experiences and the shame and fear that come with them. All these emotions and concerns working together can paralyze us.

The beautiful thing is that the gospel quiets every one of our fears. God is pleased to work in and through our fear to build his kingdom and to build confidence in us as we try to navigate these difficult conversations with wisdom.

The gospel quiets every one of our fears.

As Jesus reconciles us to God the Father, he is interested in the most intimate details of our lives. The gospel invades every area of our lives, even our bedrooms. Jesus doesn't just stand off distantly staring at us; he redeems us, transforms us, and brings healing and hope for us and our children. Sexual wholeness and healing do not come through guilt and shame or through pride and boasting in our sexual purity. There is a different and better way. We don't have to hide any longer. God uses our past experiences to make us who we are—children of the King. Our sexual past, including abuse, misuse, and lost hopes and dreams, can be very difficult to live with. But there is a God who is fundamentally good, and he has made a promise to give us "hope and a future" (Jeremiah 29:11 NIV). And this God always keeps his promises.

From Awkward to Equipped

The sex talk is awkward. You already know this is true. As parents, we don't look forward to this conversation any more than our kids do. Talking about sex is private. It is personal. We all have hang-ups, and we don't want to foist those on our kids. The conversation typically starts awkward and ends even more so.

Does the following dialogue sound familiar to you?

"Umm...honey, there is something I need to talk with you about."

Instantaneously our child thinks, *Oh no...what did I do?* "Umm... okay, what is it?"

"Umm...well, umm...do you know where babies come from and how they are made?" you say with great confidence and skill. "Well, when you are ready to talk about that, we can. But for now, let's just say that when mommies and daddies love each other, things happen and babies are born."

That's all too familiar to me!

For much of my parenting life, I (Joel) didn't know how or what to say, but now with kids in middle school, nephews and nieces in high school, and a youth group looking to me, I need a far better approach to this conversation. I need to be equipped with the story of God's good plan for sex. I need to have a good word to speak into the lives of kids who have been exposed to sexuality too early or even molested. We all need to learn what to say to our kids about sex and human sexuality—and how to say it.

All too often we start out on the wrong foot. We are far more interested in telling our kids what they absolutely cannot do than we are in showing them the goodness of sex. We are more interested in not having a sexually active kid and feeling the shame that brings on a family than we are in restoring our sexually active children to the redeeming power of the cross and the empty tomb.

Jessica and I are absolutely convinced that Jesus redeems sexually broken people, and we want you to join us on a trip through the Bible in order to see God's good plan for loving sexually broken people, making them whole again, and using them to build his kingdom. We are convinced that once you get a handle on the story of sex the Bible gives us, you will begin having these conversations in a much better and more significant way.

Jesus redeems sexually broken people.

Notice that I didn't say you would be able to have *that* conversation once, and then you're good. Just as God talks to us about sex more than once in the Bible, this will be an ongoing conversation you will be equipped to have with your kids. You may be talking about the basics in the toilet-paper aisle at Walmart or while eating fro-yo at Yogurt Land. You may be finding images you hoped you would never find on your computer, or you may be helping your child understand why sex is best saved for marriage. All of these conversations will happen more frequently (and that's a good thing!) as you open up about the subject with your children.

The conversations we propose are not easy. They may seem overly complex for your kids, but that's okay! The point is to have the conversations. So take what we say and make it fit for you and your teen.

We are not experts on this, and we're doing our best to figure this out too. We are just a brother and sister trying to live life in community as we share common experiences, successes, and failures. And learning how best to lead our kids to Christ in the midst of our sexually topsy-turvy world.

Jessica has three kids—Wesley, Hayden, and Allie. Joel has two kids—Eowyn and Colin. We've learned a lot while raising these kids… and we're still learning. We will share with you our successes and failures in our conversations with our own children and in our work with children in our churches.

A Plan for the Book

In this book, we will take a bit of a journey to discover what the Bible says about sex and sexuality as well as what the culture is saying. Every chapter ends with "Words for Moms" written by Jessica and "Words for Dads" written by Joel. These sections are not scripts for you to rehearse, but guidelines to help you in your conversations.

The book contains three parts that are easy to follow. In part 1, we look at some of the main stories and themes in Scripture and then draw out practical implications for how to talk with kids about sex. Part 2 helps you understand the cultural influences that are pressing on our kids and equips you to talk with your kids about those influences. Part 3 gets down to the nitty-gritty of the conversations and shows how to infuse them with hope.

If you picked up this book because you are in a desperate situation, first put the book down and pray that God will give you strength and hope through the marvelous power of his grace. Then skip to the chapter that you think will be most applicable for you. Don't feel the pressure to read through the whole thing if you are in the middle of a crisis. But when you can, come back later and take the time to read the whole book. You and your kids will benefit from it.

Throughout the book our hope is to give you good conversation starters with your kids. The truth of the matter is these conversations will most likely occur when you least expect or want them to. Be open to that. Start listening now for your kids to talk about sex or even hint about it, and then jump in. Thank them if they ever bring sex up to you. Be open with them.

So are you ready to see how the good news of the gospel changes the way we talk and interact with our kids about sex? If so, turn the page, and let's get started.

Part 1

Sex and the Bible

1

The Creation of Sex and Identity
When Sex Started

*The man and his wife were both
naked and were not ashamed.*
GENESIS 2:25

John and Darla have been married for 13 years. They both grew up in very strict Christian homes. John remained a virgin until they were married, but Darla had several sexual partners before she met John. She had hidden her promiscuity from her family and was active in her youth group and church. She had always been filled with shame over her decisions, and she came to view sex as something that was wrong. She also associated sex with feelings of being used.

Darla had been honest with John about this before they were married. John had initially looked down on Darla because he had been able to wait and was upset that she hadn't done the same. This only increased Darla's deep feelings of shame and regret. John forgave her, but almost every sexual experience they shared ended with Darla feeling sad and John feeling frustrated. After a few years of marriage, they decided they needed to go to a counselor together to address the situation.

Right away the counselor saw their distorted attitudes about sex.

John came into the marriage considering himself sexually pure because he had never had intercourse. Darla came into the marriage considering herself less than and used up. They both needed to hear the gospel. John needed to be reminded that the self-control he displayed in his sex life before his marriage did not make him a better person than Darla. He had viewed sex as dangerous and was scared of the consequences of being caught. Darla had also viewed sex as dangerous, but she craved the love and attention of boys more than she feared the consequences of being caught. She had used boys for attention and been used by them for sexual enjoyment.

The counselor explained to them that sex was indeed a good thing. He told them that their identities were determined not by their sexual history but rather by the love and acceptance of their good Father. They both heard for the first time that sexual pleasure wasn't something to be embarrassed about but rather something to be pursued and enjoyed.

After a few months of counseling, John and Darla began to believe these truths, and their sex life was transformed. They both started to anticipate the time together, and they found true enjoyment in pleasing each other. Sex became enjoyable for both Darla and John. He stopped thinking that Darla owed him something because of her sexual past, and she stopped feeling as if he expected her to perform. They began to delight in each other's bodies. They laughed and played with each other. Sex wasn't something to be embarrassed about or dreaded. Darla and John were able to put their past behind them and live in the freeing truth that sex was created by God for them to enjoy.

What's the big deal about sex anyway? Why is it that everyone keeps talking about it? Has it always been that way, or do we just live in an overly sexualized world? What is a healthy view of sex? Is it as important as the culture says it is? Is it as important as the church says it is? And if it is important to the church, why is it only mentioned in hushed tones?

Our concern is that teens who grow up in the church are not given a biblical view of sex. Somehow, our teens seem to get the impression they ought to fear it, to consider their bodies as shameful, and to believe that waiting now somehow earns a good sex life in marriage. In short, they are taught that sex is both good and bad.

We are also concerned that teens are looking to the world to inform their views on sex. The world teaches them that being sexually fulfilled is the most important thing. It teaches them that sex isn't such a big deal and that they should be able to have sex with whomever they like. In short, they have been taught that sex is both too important and not that important at all. John and Darla both had wrong views of sex as teenagers, and that carried into their marriage. John thought his supposed innocence made him better than Darla. Darla thought her promiscuity somehow made her less than John. Both, just like most of our teens, had a wrong view of sexual activity. Their confusion and their sinful tendencies were destroying their sex life as a married couple.

Joel's Story

When I (Joel) was growing up, I thought about sex *a lot*. Was it good? Was it as good as everyone says? Was it as good as the movies portrayed? Or was it dirty and shameful? Was it not to be enjoyed? Was it okay to think about? I didn't know, and I certainly wasn't going to ask, because that would mean I thought about sex, and my impression at the time was that I shouldn't think about it. No one explicitly taught me that message, but it was everywhere in the context I grew up in. The only time sex was discussed was when I heard about how I needed to abstain, how I needed to control my thought life, and how once you screwed up it affected everything about your future. Adults typically talked about sex negatively. My friends and I joked about sex, but it always felt forbidden.

I didn't know who to talk to about my questions. I cannot remember having *the talk* with anyone growing up, although I'm sure I did. On one hand, all I had were TV shows, movies, and music saying I should have sex. On the other hand, my parents, my pastors, and the church were telling kids like me to avoid it at all costs. I heard sex is good from the former and sex is bad from the latter. All my friends talked as if they knew what sex was, and I had a vague idea, but the only thing I knew for sure was that I was receiving mixed messages.

The church and the culture each placed significant importance on sex but on opposite sides of the same coin. The culture screamed, "Sex is everything, and if you don't participate, you are missing out and something is wrong with you." The church screamed, "Sex is everything, and if you don't wait, you are a disappointment and something is wrong with you."

The culture screamed, "Sex is everything, and if you don't participate, you are missing out and something is wrong with you." The church screamed, "Sex is everything, and if you don't wait, you are a disappointment and something is wrong with you."

Jessica's Story

I (Jessica) felt a lot of the same confusion Joel did. I vaguely remember having *the talk*, and I also remember one church class in which our pastor's wife talked to the youth about sex. I don't remember much of what she said (which is no big surprise because I can barely remember my own kids' names), and it didn't have much impact on my life.

I went to a True Love Waits conference for a day with a bunch of youth from my school. Ironically, I learned more about sex in the van ride on the way as each of the kids I was with recounted their sexual history. I remember standing up to take the pledge because everyone else did. There was no real conviction, and I am sure the youth leaders were making notes about the kids who remained in their seats. They were probably thinking, *Must remember to talk to Nicole's, Nathan's, Mike's, and Trevor's parents.*

I remember feeling like the pretty girls had a power the rest of us didn't have. I thought that if I could somehow make myself more available to boys, I could have that power too. Of course, the problem is that if you are going to use sex to gain power or approval or worth, you will end up being used. We tend to think boys are the only ones who use sex for personal gain, but I know that I used their desire to gain control over them. It isn't pretty, and it isn't what God intended.

Is the present time any different from any other time before it? Well, yes and no. Yes, our teens have access to and can be exposed to sexually explicit content in ways that were not possible before. There are scenes on cable TV that should make us blush. Men and women talk explicitly about sex in music, and art and literature are both sexualized. The popularity of *50 Shades of Grey* speaks to the desire for mainstream erotic literature.

The church is not immune to this desire, and although we clean it up in our Christian romance novels, readers are looking for the same basic thing—love, welcome, desire. Christian Amish romance novels sell more than any other Christian genre.

> As of 2014, the inspiration/religious category generated an estimated $720 million in sales a year, according to the Romance Writers of America Association, making it the third most profitable genre after crime novels, which notched just above it, and erotica, which hit nearly $1.5 billion during the same period.[1]

You can't walk through a mall without seeing sexually explicit pictures. You can't stand in line at the grocery store without headlines about sex calling to you from the magazines. There seems to be no safe place in society, and if we are honest, there is no safe place even in our own hearts. Our teens' sexual desires are amplified because of the sexual content readily available everywhere. They feel it every time they open up a social media app. They feel it every time they walk through the mall. They feel it every time their minds wander. Even if we take all of these outward things away from them or somehow try to protect them, they will still feel sexual desire. We were made to feel sexual desire. Sexual desire isn't what is wrong with us.

We were made to feel sexual desire.
Sexual desire isn't what is wrong with us.

But when we come to the Bible, we find out that sex has been on people's minds all along. It has been said before that if the Bible were made into a movie that followed the text closely, it would be R-rated at least. Sex, violence, betrayal, more sex, more violence...but even still, all throughout its pages the beautiful story of redemption rings out in every circumstance. From Genesis to Revelation, sex is a big deal.

The goodness of sex is something the church has shied away from. We want our teens to stay away from it in thought, word, and deed, but maybe that contributes to the fact that 80 percent of evangelical young adults (ages 18 to 29) admit to having premarital sex.[2] We think that if we just tell of the dangers and of the need to abstain, we will somehow turn off their sexual desire. The problem is, that is not working, and we are leaving out the most important part of sex—it's *goodness*. History teaches us that we cannot dissuade people from an act just by telling them it is bad. We need to give them something better. What we hope to communicate in this chapter is that God made sex and the sexes, and everything he made is good.

Sex and Creation

> *God blessed them. And God said to them,*
> *"Be fruitful and multiply and fill the earth."*
> GENESIS 1:28

"In the beginning..." These three words start us out on an amazing journey. They are brimming with potential and hope. We read these at the beginning of the creation account, where God sets his plan of redemption into action. In the first two chapters of the Bible, we find out where we came from and how God pulled the whole thing off (by the power of his word).

God created man with specific intentions in mind, and he told his creation what they were to do—work, subdue, and fill. For work, he gave Adam tasks and rest. For subduing, he gave Adam the right to name. And for filling, he gave Adam a companion, Eve. Adam looked around the Garden and at all the creatures and realized he was alone. Yes, he had God, but God and Adam could not fulfill the mandate to be fruitful and multiply unless God spoke more beings into life. So God gave Eve to Adam, and when he did, God looked at everything and said, "It is very good!"

But what is most important for our discussion is that when God created Adam and Eve and set them in the Garden, he gave them a mandate to have sex, and he deemed it "very good." Just think about what a hopeful event that is. Our most private and vulnerable moments were created by God for us to enjoy! And creation was not complete, it was not very good, until Adam and Eve shared this intimate bond.

This is how we can affirm the goodness of pleasure. God has hardwired us to enjoy the pleasures of sex. He is so kind to create our bodies so that our centers of nerves are meant for pleasure. God has designed our bodies to work in such a way that when those areas are stimulated, chemicals are released in our brains that indicate pleasure. We are hardwired to enjoy sex, and it is good! It is not shameful to have sex for fun. Sex was God's idea to begin with. In his all-knowing, all-loving design, he made us to desire and enjoy sex. There was nothing shameful or embarrassing about it. Adam and Eve surely enjoyed sex to the fullest.

Sex was God's idea to begin with.

God affirms the value of both sexes, and our physiology does as well. God has made both male and female in his image. Both have incredible value because of this. There is no sense in which Adam is more of the image of God than Eve. They are equally made in God's image. And again, God has hardwired their bodies to be different and to reflect that difference. It is down to the very core of who they are biologically. There is no way that Adam could confuse this. The physical differences were remarkable, and were made to enjoy.

Male and female were made to serve the other sexually. They didn't try to take advantage of each other sexually, emotionally, or in any other way. Women are not objects for men to use to get their jollies. Men are not beasts who cannot control themselves once they start to get aroused. Both male and female are created by God and called good—there is no superior sex. Both are named and known by God intimately. They know each other, naked and unashamed. Love for God and love for each other was the theme of every day and every night.

Sex Is Extraordinary: It Was *Good*

God saw everything that he had made, and behold, it was very good.

GENESIS 1:31

Only after Adam and Eve were together and sharing intimacy was creation complete and "very good." That word "good" means morally and aesthetically pleasing. Once man and woman were created, God leaned back and declared that the two of them looked good together on the inside and the outside. They were completely whole, lacking nothing.

The Bible describes Adam and Eve as "naked and unashamed." This isn't just a physical descriptor but an emotional one as well. They had nothing to hide from each other—no sexual secrets, no sexual past, no selfish desires. They were completely and unabashedly uncovered before one another and before God. They felt no shame in the act of sex before God. They needed nothing to cover them physically and nothing to cover them emotionally. They were perfect in each other's eyes and before God.

At times my (Jessica's) spouse tells me that my body is perfect. But he is not blind—he sees all my imperfections. His choice to overlook my imperfections is the purest act of love. Adam and Eve did not suffer from a broken self-image. They didn't need to turn off the lights or try to maintain some physical or emotional facade of perfection. They were able to be united as one because there was nothing between them. They were not ashamed of their bodies—they delighted in each other so completely, there was no reason to feel shame. There was no comparison, no unrealistic standard of beauty. They both were who they were created to be.

When God first created humanity, there were no barriers

to a harmonious and pleasurable relationship—sexually, emotionally, psychologically, and spiritually. Because they had a harmonious relationship with God, they had a harmonious relationship with each other. They were in the Garden naked and enjoying each other. We can presume this meant not only enjoying one another's bodies sexually, but also enjoying the companionship of intimately exploring creation together.[3]

This idea of naked and unashamed is not only how they felt before others but also how they felt before God, and it is the key to understanding and having good sex—it must first come from a right relationship with God. You are able to have *physically* fulfilling sex apart from a relationship with God, but you are not able to have *completely* fulfilling sex apart from a right relationship with God. In order for you to emotionally, physically, and spiritually enjoy sex, you must be in right relationship with your Creator.

The Bible consistently affirms that when sex is confined to marriage, it is very good. Dan Allender underscores this in his book *God Loves Sex*.

> God loves sex. He conceived, created, and blessed the process by which our bodies know and are known through desire, arousal, foreplay, intercourse, orgasm, and rest.
>
> Sex is meant by God to be one of the bridge experiences between earth and heaven. It awakens and intersects our deepest physical and spiritual desires. Sex, like music, fills us simultaneously with notes of an intense immanent bodily pleasure and with the sonorous reverberations of another world that is transcendent and holy.[4]

God called sex good. He saw the union of Adam and Eve and was happy about it. He loved Adam and Eve (and you and me!) so much that he gave us this amazing gift.

The entire book of Song of Solomon is dedicated to the goodness of sex in marriage. It celebrates the joy of arousal and playful interaction. Proverbs 5:19 commands, "Let her breasts fill you at all times with delight; be intoxicated always in her love." The words "delight" and "intoxicated" give us permission to enjoy sex. Sex is good. This is a message that we all need to hear. It isn't dirty to have sex! It isn't dirty to long for your spouse! God loves pleasure. Pleasure is not innately bad—it was God's idea to begin with. When we enjoy sex, we are actually doing what we were created to do.

You might be rolling your eyes and thinking, *How in the world do I talk to my kids about the goodness of sex without making them want it right now?* The truth is, if they are approaching the teenage years, they probably already want it right now. At the very least, they are curious. The desire for sexual activity isn't a bad thing. We were created with a desire to experience sex. We can't let fear dictate our conversations with our children. We must let love and trust in God guide the way. It is better for your children for you to lead this conversation than to ignore it. Pray and trust God to use your words to engender a good and holy desire for sex.

God Created Identity

God created man in his own image, in the image of God he created him; male and female he created them.
Genesis 1:27

This may be the first time in history that we have defined personhood by our sexual desires. We have been defined by many other things, including race, class, level of schooling, work, and religion. When cultures have used these external matters to define personhood, the inevitable result is oppression and pain. Think of the caste system in India, slavery in Western Europe and the United States, wars between Islam and Christianity in the Middle East, and the treatment of Jews in Europe during the 1940s. Whenever humanity has used anything other than our core humanness to define personhood, people are dehumanized. Those who hold the power consider themselves superior and oppress those they consider inferior.

When God created male and female in his image, he gave us value and worth that transcend any of these external markers. He values each human and knows each of us by name, not by our sexuality. When we give our sexuality the pride of place and allow it to define our identity as human beings, we make too big of a deal out of sex. Jenell Williams Paris says, "When such a big deal is made of it, sex becomes an idol, offering identity and purpose to individuals and economic growth and international notoriety to nations. Sex is not such a big deal and it deserves to be dethroned."[5]

This shift in our understanding of the importance of sex is shown in the discussion of sexual identity. Not until the 2000s was our sexuality defined by our desires. We have elevated the role of our sexual desires to the point that they define our identity. The problem with this is that our desires are trumping our DNA. What we *feel like* we are is taking the place of what we are scientifically and genetically. We are exchanging the way God made us for the way we want ourselves to be made, trading God's image for our own.

Of course, some people just don't feel right in their own skin—men who feel feminine, women who feel masculine—and they don't have the place or the space to be able to explore those feelings. As a result, they often feel condemned and categorized by others. The woman who feels like a man, loves construction, dresses in a masculine way, enjoys the company of women over men, and has no desire to marry a man is automatically labeled as a lesbian by those in her family, church, or friend group. This should not be. Our outward appearance, our actions, or even our inward desires do not define who we are.

Sexual desires and orientation don't make you who you are. When we degrade our identity to our sexuality or sexual feelings, we give in to something lesser—our base desires. We are letting an idol become our god.

> Sin inverts love for God, which in turn becomes idolatry, and inverts love for neighbor, which becomes exploitation. Instead of worshiping God, our inclination becomes to worship anything but God. Idolatry is not the ceasing of worship. Rather, it is misdirected worship, and at the core of idolatry is self-worship.[6]

When we turn our sexual desires or sexual identity into our god, we will end up heartbroken. Our true identity comes from what God has done for us through his Son, Jesus Christ.

> Our true identity comes from what God has
> done for us through his Son, Jesus Christ.

Building a Christ-centered identity in our children is ultimately the work of the Holy Spirit, but as parents we can weave this theme into the fabric of our parenting. The good news of what Christ has done for us and our children declares that we no longer have to find our identity in what we do, how we perform, or even whom we desire. Our identity comes from the finished work of Christ.

We need to repeat this good news to our children in their success and in their failures. When they do well in school, on the field, in something they create, or in a performance of some sort, let's celebrate their success but in a way that builds their true identity on Christ, not on their accomplishments. That can be as simple as telling them that you are so excited to watch them grow and learn but that ultimately the best news about them is what Christ has done for them. And in their failures, we can be sure to tell them they aren't defined by what they do wrong, but by the love of God.

In 2 Corinthians 12:10, Paul talks about contentedness: "For the sake of Christ, then, I am content with weaknesses, insults, hardships, persecutions, and calamities. For when I am weak, then I am strong." It can be a hardship to be content with who God has made us, but in that very space of weakness and calamity we can learn that the power of God rests on us in our weakness. These verses are not talking about how strong Paul is; they show that when we admit our weakness, we make room for the power of God to rest on us.

Because our identity, our true human self, is deeper than our desires or feelings, we can learn to be content. And because our true human self, our image-bearing self, is loved, forgiven, and counted as righteous, we can rejoice even in our weakness. We can draw strength from knowing that our identity is not based on what we do or don't do. It's not defined by whom we desire or whom we don't desire. Rather, our identity is based on what Christ did for us. Our identity is founded, rooted, and grounded in the saving work of the Son, and nothing we can do will change that. That is where our contentment comes from. It doesn't come from living out our own desires; it comes from God's desire to make us his children.

God and Sex

Our sexuality affirms the love that the Trinity has for us. We give of ourselves, we experience joy together, we desire what is good for the other person...and it is good! The love that exists in the Trinity is often described as a self-giving dance in which the members of the Trinity affirm love for each by living for each other's joy. This is a mystery that we cannot classify or explain easily because God is God and we are not. But when we see the interplay between the Father, the Son, and the Holy Spirit in the New Testament, we get a sense of how this works. The Father sends the Son (John 6:38; Romans 8:3; Galatians 4:4). The Son's desire, his food, is to do all that the Father has sent him to do (John 4:34; 14:31; Hebrews 10:7). And the Father and the Son send the Spirit (John 17; Galatians 4:6).[7]

Our sex can be shaped and changed by this fundamental reality. We emulate the love the members of the Trinity have for one another when we give of ourselves sexually to bring pleasure to our spouse. We delight in what our partner delights in. We love bringing pleasure. We learn to love finding what brings the other joy. As we delight, love, and find secret pleasures, we learn to celebrate differences. We can smile at how much joy we give our partner. The give-and-take in our sexual relationship is meant to point us to the higher reality of finding happiness in others' happiness, not in self-pleasure or self-worship. Of course, the members of the Trinity are not sexually involved with each other, but the love they share is something that ought to shape our love for our spouse.

We affirm one God in three persons. This is not a perfect analogy, but we do know that God is a united God. God shares a common essence, the same substance, and each member of the Trinity is united to the other. Sex affirms our union with one another. The complete giving of ourselves during sex is meant to reflect our oneness. We physically become one flesh. The hope and the goal is that we become one emotionally and spiritually as well. This becoming one is a reflection of Adam and Eve being "naked and unashamed" in the Garden. And although now our brokenness hinders us from completely enjoying oneness to the fullest, we do experience it in an unparalleled way during sex. That oneness should be displayed in a matched excitement in giving and receiving pleasure. Sex is so much more than a physical act; it is a joining of one to another.

> Sex is so much more than a physical act;
> it is a joining of one to another.

Our sexuality also affirms Christ's love for his people. The Old Testament refers to God as a husband and Israel as his (often unfaithful) bride. "Your Maker is your husband, the LORD of hosts is his name; and the Holy One of Israel is your Redeemer, the God of the whole earth he is called" (Isaiah 54:5). And of course, in the New Testament, the church is called the bride of Christ (Ephesians 5:22-32). Something in our sexual union in marriage displays Christ's love for his bride, the church!

Sex Is Ordinary: No Hidden Mystery

As I (Joel) was growing up, sex was a taboo subject around our Christian friends. We all thought about sex, but we were ashamed to admit it. So sex became a mystery. We didn't have computers or smartphones or the internet. Instead, we had magazines that were kept behind the counter. Sex was hidden because it was dirty (we thought), and only the dirty people looked at those magazines. Only the dirty people talked about it, and only the dirty people had sex.

As Jessica and I have grown older, we have seen how damaging this mentality can be. Many people carry the weight of feeling dirty because of their past. I have friends who left the church because they felt like outsiders after having premarital sex. Others feel less than because they have been molested. In fact, that was my own experience. I long for people to know the freedom of forgiveness regardless of their sexual history.

The availability of sexual content today is affecting our teens in ways we don't yet fully comprehend. We know from several scientific studies that the use of porn changes the brain.[8] But we have not yet grasped how it changes our kids emotionally. The destruction that porn inflicts on a person's life is a well-proven fact, but with smartphones and the internet, we probably haven't seen the full consequences of living in a sex-saturated society. Our kids are living with temptations and pressures we can't even begin to understand. We talk about that more in part 2 of this book.

Sex is extraordinary in that it unites us to another person, and yet it is also very ordinary. We were meant to experience that sort of intimacy, union, and pleasure. But in our culture, sex has become so ordinary as to be devalued.

Instead of falling into extremes, let's bring sex into its proper place. Let's talk to our kids about its goodness when it is enjoyed in the proper context. Let's give them a view of sex that emphasizes how it gives value to our spouse and displays our love for them. In short, let's talk about the ordinary beauty of sex as it was created by God.

Again, we understand this is a difficult conversation. We understand the fears of saying too much or saying too little, of our words coming out wrong, of hurting our children. We will say it again: Don't let your fear control you. Pray, ask the Lord for wisdom, and trust that he will use your words according to his will. Fear is a liar. Fear tells you that if you don't get the conversation just right, you will do more harm than good. But we don't have to fear. We can be honest with our kids, admit our fears, and then affirm that even in our fears we trust God with their hearts. We don't have to act as if we have it all together. Our kids don't need us to pretend we know everything. Our kids need our honesty and our wisdom. So share what you have learned and trust your heavenly Father with your kids' hearts and minds.

Words for Dads

Dad, in these sections of the book, I (Joel) want to give you some ideas for conversation starters. I am not going to tell you what to say. I have faith that the Holy Spirit is at work in you and is giving you the wisdom to turn this potentially awkward conversation into an ongoing, life-giving exchange. So can I encourage you? Don't check out. This isn't Mom's discussion. Distorted views of sex flourish when men remove themselves from the parenting picture. Mom doesn't know what it is like to be a man and to wrestle with our particular struggles. You know what it is like to have insatiable appetites, body parts acting oddly, feelings of pressure to go out and sow your seed, and friends talking about sex. You know the seemingly unstoppable desire to have sex, and my guess is you know what it is like to turn to things like pornography when you are weak.

So don't check out. Take up your calling from God. It's not too late to teach your children about sex. In the best way possible, "Be strong, and show yourself a man" (1 Kings 2:2). God has given you the blessing of being able to say things to your children that Mom cannot say, to be able to talk to your daughter about how beautiful she is and to your son about holding on, resisting the culture around him.

Your children need you to help them think about the world in a way that honors God and responds out of love for what Christ has done. Your past does not define you. You may think that since you have sinned sexually, you have no leg to stand on. You may have experienced porn addiction, premarital sex, or some of the identity issues we discussed earlier. Let me assure you that God has placed you where you need to be and that he is willing and able to forgive you. If you struggle with any of these issues, I encourage you to run to Christ for forgiveness and then go to a trusted pastor or counselor who can walk with you into wholeness and freedom. There is hope!

Perhaps you have been broken sexually through abuse (as I have). If so, I am so sorry that you have had to carry that shame. What was done to you was wrong. It should never have happened, and it was not your fault. I know this is an incredibly difficult subject to work through, but there is hope and restoration at the cross. Let me assure you that even in your brokenness, Christ is making you whole again through the power of the Spirit. You are special to him, and he will never abuse you. You are useful for the kingdom, and this incredibly important task of talking to your children about sex is part of your kingdom work.

Your children need to see and hear that you are a human being with struggles like theirs and that you need grace and hope, just as they do. Talk to them about God's good creation and design of sex. Don't shy away. Take a minute to ask God to give you strength to lovingly approach your children and begin this lifelong conversation about sex and sexuality.

Words for Moms

It would be really easy to let your mistakes or hurts define your view of sex and shape your conversations with your kids about it. Because our intellect is tainted by sin, it is important to let the Bible define sex. It is good; it is meant to be pleasurable; it isn't dirty.

But you may have been used sexually and even abused, so to you I want to say first that I am sorry for what happened to you. It was not your fault. You are not to blame for any type of abuse that was inflicted upon you last week or decades ago. What was done to you was wrong. I can understand wanting to hide or deny what happened, but I do hope you will talk with a trusted individual who can walk with you and support you in this pain even if it happened a long time ago. You deserve more than to live in silence. You may believe you can teach your children the right views of sex without dealing with what has happened to you, but it will benefit you and your children if you are able to receive counseling and to receive the help and comfort you need.

I also understand that you may be afraid to share not only what has happened to you but also what you have done. What your sexual history says about you should always take a backseat to what the Bible says about you. You are free to share with your children (in an age-appropriate way) about your past sexual struggles. If your kids think you have always had it together and have been a perfect Christian with no sexual struggles, then they won't feel comfortable coming to you with their own struggles. The beauty of the gospel is that God redeems every part of the believer's life. He can take the ugliest parts and change them into lovely markers of his redemptive grace.

We can affirm the goodness of sex to our teens by being careful about the words we use. We can affirm the goodness of sex in our simple actions—for example, enjoying our husband's playful advances. I understand that there might be a lot to deal with inside a marriage, but if we truly believe the Bible is our standard, we will affirm that sex, the way God created it to be, is good. We can tell our kids about the goodness of sex without being inappropriately explicit. We can tell them about the power of sex—how it can unite and heal. We can tell them that sexual pleasure is not a bad thing, but rather a really, really good thing. We can tell them they were meant to enjoy sex. So when our children experience sexual feelings, instead of shaming them out of them, we can tell them that their bodies were created to feel those things. Then we can share with them how God wants to maximize that pleasure appropriately.

As we talk to our children about sex, let's not just talk about the "how to" aspect of it. Let's talk about the pleasure that is involved, the happiness it should create, the unity it inspires, the gratefulness to God it engenders in our hearts. Take back what the culture has stolen. Rather than allowing cultural influences to tell our kids how to find sexual pleasure, let's share the truth: God is the one who created sex to be pleasurable. The forbidden pleasure of sex makes it alluring, so take that part away. Tell your kids the pleasure is theirs to enjoy, and they will experience it at its fullest the way God intended them to.

When we are ashamed or embarrassed to talk to our kids about sex, they will go look for answers somewhere else. So encourage conversations about sex. It doesn't have to be embarrassing. Trust me—the more you talk about it, the easier talking about it gets. The first few times might be awkward, but the more you pursue this conversation, the more your kids will pursue you. If they don't want to talk about it, just let them know you are available.

As Joel and I have been working on this book, the topic of sex has come up a lot more around my house. I have books lying around that my kids typically wouldn't see me read. This has led to some important discussions. Our good friends have a joke with their kids—anytime the discussion of sex comes up, the family laughs about OPS (old person sex). This joke has put their kids at ease and made it a lot easier to get to the more serious parts of the conversation.

Again, I understand that deep pain may surface during this discussion, and you may feel it is not a laughing matter. Our hope in this book is that God will heal those hurts so you may also delight in the goodness of sex the way it was created to be enjoyed.

Mom, it's okay for you to talk to your boys about sex. If your husband doesn't want to have the conversation or if you don't have a husband, then by all means, talk to them. The bottom line is that you need to start the conversation. For the sake of your children, take that faltering, uncomfortable step. Put aside your personal comfort and love your kiddos. Don't leave their knowledge of sex to the internet or to their friends. Give them the full, robust news that sex is a good thing, created by God to be enjoyed.

And it's okay to smile when you tell them that.

TALKING POINTS

- God created sex, and it is good.

- God is our Creator. He has given us our identity, and it is good.

- The love we express in sex is a self-giving love. It mirrors the love the members of the Trinity have for one another.

2

Stories of Sexual Brokenness and God's Redemption
When Sex Broke

Everyone who looks at a woman with lustful intent has already committed adultery with her in his heart.

MATTHEW 5:28

Marcia first went to counseling because of her overeating problem. She was about 100 pounds overweight. Although she had gone to her physician and had tried multiple diets, she just couldn't seem to overcome her compulsion to eat. She also seemed unhappy with her relationships in general and her marriage in particular.

As Marcia's counselor sought to understand her problems and the issues she faced, she was touched by Marcia's suffering and sorrows. Marcia was a victim of child abuse. Her divorced mother, who had been promiscuous while Marcia was young, had married a man who was to become Marcia's abuser. At first, she enjoyed her relationship with him as he flattered her with dolls and special favors, and she grew to trust him. He began touching and kissing her, and although she felt uncomfortable, he assured her this was a normal relationship for a daughter and stepfather "who really loved each other."

This secret activity became more and more pronounced and Marcia, at age 12, found herself functioning in the role of her mother. She was the caretaker. She was the lover. Her brother, Adam, was terribly abused by both her mother and stepfather, being beaten with belts and locked in closets. Although Marcia felt badly for him, she was confident she wouldn't have these same problems because she was "special."

Marcia was experiencing a double tragedy: Her stepfather used and manipulated her while her mother, who should have protected her, turned a blind eye.

As time went on, Marcia and Adam found life more and more unbearable. They were not allowed to call anyone on the phone, go to friends' homes, or invite anyone over after school. Frequently they missed school because their parents needed them to stay home and care for things in the family business. If they failed to be compliant, both their mother and stepfather punished them. Marcia's complaints about their situation earned her a three-month summer vacation in her room. During this time she was allowed visits only from her brother and stepfather.

Marcia and Adam tried to figure out how to please their parents. In humiliation, Marcia became a doormat, increasingly seeking ways to comply with her parents. Because Adam was angrier, he gave up trying to please and developed a defiant and rebellious lifestyle. Marcia became increasingly aware that her physical relationship with her stepfather was very wrong. As she began to resist his advances, he became more and more violent, threatening to send her to a detention center if she resisted or told anyone about them. He frequently beat her brother to punish her for noncompliance.

Marcia was repeatedly raped during her teen years. Daily she faced the probability of having to unwillingly acquiesce to her stepfather's perverted demands in an attempt to purchase peace at any price. (To this day, Marcia's mother claims she was unaware of the sexual abuse.)

Although Marcia was not a Christian, she began to pray that God would help her and her brother. During this time, the Lord opened Marcia's heart and gave her faith to believe. A Christian friend at school spoke to her about Jesus, and Marcia began to experience a peace she had never known before. Marcia was 16.

She knew she had to escape her home situation. Soon, the Lord opened the door. Although Marcia had knowledge about sexual relationships that was beyond her years, she was extremely naive about the workings of the world. One afternoon, while watching television, she discovered she could make collect telephone calls. To ensure that her stepfather would not find out, she called the operator and asked if records were made of collect calls. Assured that she could make a collect call without her parents' knowledge, she found her birth father's phone number and called him. Pleading with him to keep their conversation secret, Marcia poured out her heart to him, describing the ghastly situation she and Adam were in and begging him to rescue her. He assured her that he would take care of her. For the first time in many years, Marcia went to sleep that night with hope for the future.

In school the following day, she was called to the principal's office. There she found police officers waiting for her. They informed her that her mother and stepfather had accused her of lying and being incorrigible. They asked that she be kept in juvenile detention until she could be made a ward of the state or other arrangements could be made. Marcia, who had always tried to be a good girl in school, was led out of the principal's office in handcuffs.

Crushed, despairing, and humiliated, Marcia's mind was filled with one haunting thought: Her stepfather had carried out his threat. She spent an entire month in juvenile detention, feeling like a criminal, while her mother, father, and stepfather fought over who was going to take responsibility for this rebellious troublemaker.

She eventually went to live with her grandmother, who made it clear that she only took Marcia to get her out of "jail." Marcia was thankful for a short rest. Adam had been sent to live with another relative, and she would not see him again for many years. Marcia was made to feel guilty for breaking up the family and for causing her mother trouble. Her grandmother never missed an opportunity to remind her that she had caused this difficulty and her mother's subsequent divorce. The truth became evident to Marcia—no one was going to believe her or rescue her.

As she continued going to counseling, her heart and life began to heal. Eventually, Marcia married and gave birth to three children. Both she and her husband are Christians and are seeking to serve the Lord, yet she still struggles. The deep and horrific wounds of her childhood will haunt her until she is face-to-face with her true rescuer.

True Confessions

This is one of the most difficult chapters for me (Joel) to write because this is similar to my story. When I was a young man, I was molested by a disconnected family member, and that brought unimaginable shame into my life. It gave me a skewed view of sex—that it was always and only broken and shameful. I always felt broken and shamed. This was compounded by my stumbling upon a *Playboy* magazine when I was nine years old. We weren't looking for it; we were just out playing basketball. But this gave me a broken understanding of who and what women were for. I grew up in a great Christian home with loving parents, but people experience brokenness even in homes where parents try to protect their children from stuff like this.

These two events provided a bad foundation for the understanding of sexuality I carried into my life. Over and over again I wondered, *Does God redeem sexually broken people?* In this chapter, I hope you hear the answer I have heard from my friends, my family, my pastor, and God himself through his Word: YES! When we bring our brokenness to God and lay it at the foot of the cross, he makes us whole where we have been hurt, and he forgives us where we have sinned. This is the good news of the gospel! God is pleased to work in and through sexually broken people to bring his kingdom to earth.

> When we bring our brokenness to God and lay it at the foot of the cross, he makes us whole where we have been hurt, and he forgives us where we have sinned.

It is important for our own hearts to pursue sexual healing and for us to believe these truths before we can impart the truth to our children. If you have experienced serious sexual brokenness, maybe now is the time for you to seek out counseling with a qualified individual or maybe just share your experiences with a trusted friend. At the very least it would be good to pray and ask the Lord to start to open up that part of your heart so that you may experience the healing you so desperately need. Your healing will affect how you communicate with your children about sex.

At some level, all of us have sinned or still do sin sexually. Jesus says in the Sermon on the Mount that if you lust after someone, you have committed adultery in your heart with them (Matthew 5:28). This deepening of the law shows us that merely abstaining from sex before marriage does not make you clean sexually. You are undoubtedly trying to raise your children in a sexually healthy environment, but that does not mean they are immune from sexual sin. They too either have experienced or will experience the pain of sexual sin. An influence from the outside or their own disordered desires will cause this pain. You, me, our kids…all of us need the redeeming power of the gospel to invade our sexuality and to bring about good, gospel ends, even in the bedroom of our hearts.

This story is difficult on another level. The stories we will look at in this chapter focus on dark subjects—incest, rape, prostitution, drunkenness, and violence. These are not easy stories to tell, but as we said before, the Bible never shies away from difficult stories. It is graphically honest. This is one of the ways we know the Bible is true. It does the opposite of most books by showing us all the character flaws of the protagonists. It does not hide the reality of sexual brokenness.

Sex, the Fall, and the Abuse of Power

In pain you shall bring forth children. Your desire shall be for your husband, and he shall rule over you.

GENESIS 3:16 NKJV

Lamech took two wives.

GENESIS 4:19

Sin is swift, and its destructive power is undeniable. Adam and

Eve rebelled, and since then, every human has lived in the destructive wake of that single act. Eve now desired to overthrow the good care of her husband, and her pain in childbearing increased. Adam now had to work for everything he was to have, and his labor, which was once a joy, would now be a difficult burden.

Can you imagine just for a minute what this must have been like? Adam and Eve, who knew no pain, whose relationship was perfect, whose sex was really good, now fought with each other. Those who were once naked and unashamed now hid from God and shifted the blame because it ran so deep. Add to that the promise of pain in childbearing and the toil of less fruitful work...the brokenness of sin was truly taking hold.

What was meant to be a joyous celebration of Adam and Eve's union brought pain into their lives. They had two sons, Cain and Abel (Genesis 4). Cain murdered his brother, and the destructive effects of sin continued.

One of Cain's descendants, Lamech—a petty and vengeful man—was consumed with power. He too commited murder, and we begin to see his desire to take advantage of his position and the weakness of others. Lamech took two wives, introducing a new kind of breaking down of the goodness of sex. This is the first time in the Bible that we read of the abuse of the opposite sex and of sex itself. What was meant to be a "bone of my bone" relationship became a polygamous monstrosity. In this, the seed of the serpent had set up its camp.

Sex was always meant to be a picture of the loving union that a man and a woman share. It was originally Garden-of-Eden perfect. Sex was never meant to be used to show off power and domination. It was never meant to be used for selfish gain. Part of the goodness of sex is the unity it is meant to create between a husband and wife. In Lamech's story we see the brokenness of the fall coming through.

When Shechem the son of Hamor the Hivite, the prince of the land, saw [Dinah], he seized her and lay with her and humiliated her.
GENESIS 34:2

Sadly, the brokenness did not get better; it only got worse. In

Genesis 34 (a chapter of the Bible most churches avoid like the plague), we read of the sad story of power being used again in an even more destructive way. Lamech had used his power to gain multiple wives, disregarding the goodness of sex depicted in the Garden. Here in Genesis 34, Shechem uses his political power and physical strength to overwhelm Dinah and rape her.

Rape is an unimaginably destructive abuse of power. In this instance the rape starts with improper lust and ends in the death of an entire city. Martin Luther King Jr. said, "Hate multiplies hate, violence multiplies violence…The chain reaction of evil—hate begetting hate, wars producing more wars."[1] Here we read of a perfect example of that. The violence of rape is met with the violence of murder, and the Israelites become a stench in the nostrils of the nations.

Rape is never okay. The victim of rape is never to blame. No matter how the victim dresses, how drunk the victim gets, or what sort of tenuous situation the victim enters, he or she is never to blame for another person misusing power to take advantage.

Though we use our sexuality to gain power over others, Jesus never did. Husbands and wives may force their will or withhold sex for selfish reasons, but Jesus gives himself perfectly. He never uses his power for his own pleasure or to gain an unlawful advantage over humanity. In fact, he did the exact opposite—he used his power to serve the powerless by setting it aside and becoming a man. In doing this, Jesus redeems both the rape victim and rapist. In this way, Jesus repairs our broken sexuality, cares for the disadvantaged, and changes the sinner.

Sex, Sex Trafficking, and the Prostitute

He may lie with you tonight in exchange for your son's mandrakes.
GENESIS 30:15

Please identify whose these are, the signet and the cord and the staff.
GENESIS 38:25

Joshua the son of Nun sent two men secretly from Shittim as spies, saying, "Go, view the land, especially Jericho." And they went and came into the house of a prostitute whose name was Rahab and lodged there.

Joshua 2:1

The Bible is not shy. The Bible is not coy. The Bible is not Victorian and prudish when it comes to sex. But the Bible is not overly explicit either. God always gives us just enough detail to get our minds thinking along the right track so we can understand what God is doing in the world—redeeming us from our sin. Let me encourage you to take a break right now. Take out your Bible and read these three accounts (Genesis 30, Genesis 38, and Joshua 2). Go ahead. We'll wait.

Now, with all of that crazy stuff swimming in your minds, what do you see? As I (Joel) sit here and read about these situations, the sun is rising over the mountains just outside my window, and the clouds look as though they are set on fire. Here we have four incredibly broken situations, and yet they point to God's care for his people and provision of a Redeemer. There is no mistaking it: God brings the Messiah through broken people and to broken people. He enters an ugly situation (that gets even worse) and brings beauty from it. He sees a hopeless situation and brings the hope of the nations. Let's briefly trace this in each account.

Rachel, Leah, and Jacob

First, Rachel, Leah, and Jacob. This is one of the saddest stories of the Bible. Nobody wanted poor weak-eyed Leah, but her father tricked Jacob into marrying her in a sort of two-for-one deal. Her sister Rachel, the favorite wife, was beautiful, but after the wedding, she was bitter because of infertility. Rachel and Leah used Jacob to gain power over each other. Jacob slept with the wife who happened to come his way. This family was a hot mess. Here in Genesis 30, we see just how out of control things have gotten.

Rachel knows Jacob loves her more than he loves Leah, but Leah is the only one producing children. The bitterness between the two of them is oozing off the page. But God's mercy will not be stopped, and we see how it begins to shine through. Listen to this business deal.

In the days of wheat harvest Reuben went and found mandrakes in the field and brought them to his mother Leah. Then Rachel said to Leah, "Please give me some of your son's mandrakes." But she said to her, "Is it a small matter that you have taken away my husband? Would you take away my son's mandrakes also?" Rachel said, "Then he may lie with you tonight in exchange for your son's mandrakes." When Jacob came from the field in the evening, Leah went out to meet him and said, "You must come in to me, for I have hired you with my son's mandrakes." So he lay with her that night. And God listened to Leah, and she conceived and bore Jacob a fifth son. Leah said, "God has given me my wages because I gave my servant to my husband." So she called his name Issachar (Genesis 30:14-18).

How could anything good come from a situation like this? If God gave us what we deserved, if God handed out blessing only when his people acted properly, he could never use or redeem this situation. But the beauty is that he did. Rachel's womb was opened, and she conceived and bore Joseph, who would deliver his whole family, including his brother Judah, a forefather of Christ. Out of this dire situation—the selling of a man for sex, polygamy, and the bitterness of two sisters—God brings the Savior. Through this more than dysfunctional and unloving familial situation, the Loving One would come forth and bring his children into his family.

Judah and Tamar

Next, we see Judah and Tamar (Genesis 38). This is a very troublesome story, but again we read of how God cares for women and uses broken sexuality to bring about salvation for the world. Judah's firstborn son, Er, marries Tamar. Now Er was a bad guy, so he died. Then Judah gave Tamar to his second son, Onan, as was the custom at the time, so that Er's name could continue. But every time Onan and Tamar had sex, Onan would practice coitus interruptus and "waste the semen on the ground" (Genesis 38:9). He used Tamar for sex but didn't give her a child who would provide for her in the future. So God put Onan to death as well.

A third son, Shelah, is next in line to marry Tamar and carry on his brother Er's lineage, but Judah is scared and does not want Shelah to die. So he does what any reasonable man would do—he disobeys God's laws and does not give Shelah to Tamar. He continues to provide financially for Tamar but will not give her the satisfaction of having a husband.

Now the story goes from bad to worse. Tamar finds out that Judah is going on a trip, so she disguises herself as a cult prostitute and waits along the way for him. He sees her, hires her, and uses her for his own sexual pleasure. He isn't smart enough to practice coitus interruptus, and she gets pregnant. Had Er and Onan learned to use women sexually from their father Judah?

Judah isn't carrying any money, so he tries to strike a bargain, but he gives up the very things that would eventually identify him as the father—his ring, staff, and cord. Judah was at least an honest John, so he eventually sent payment. But the prostitute is nowhere to be found, so he tries to cover up his sin and save his reputation, forgetting the whole incident.

As tends to happen, Tamar starts to show, and Judah is not very happy with his daughter-in-law. In fact, he is going to have her burned to death. But Tamar sends the very signs of Judah's sin—the ring, cord, and staff—and says, "By the man to whom these belong, I am pregnant... Please identify whose these are, the signet and the cord and the staff" (Genesis 38:25). Judah was had, and he knew it. He said, "She is more righteous than I, since I did not give her my son Shelah" (verse 26).

Now, we could read a story like this and totally miss the point by saying, "Oh, buuurrrnn." But this was more than a great burn set up by a God who cares for women and has an amazing sense of irony. It is a story of redemption! Tamar gives birth to Perez and Zerah. Why is that important? When you flip in your Bible to Matthew 1:3, you read this little line in the genealogy of Christ: "And Judah the father of Perez and Zerah by Tamar, and Perez the father of Hezron." There are only five women mentioned in the genealogy of Jesus. One of them is Tamar.

Yes, this Tamar. The one who has sex with her father-in-law. Right there at the beginning of the genealogy of Christ we read of God bringing about salvation through this broken situation. But God used this terrible situation so that you and I could be saved. The scandal is that there is no sin that can disqualify you from being included in the King of Love's plan of redemption. The scandal is that God looks at all our sin— even the sexual ones—and declares us righteous because of the work of Christ. When I read this, my heart leaps for joy! God cares for us all!

Rahab

We want to point out one more story that shows us that God cares for people who are sexually broken. Rahab, a prostitute who was not an Israelite, was an unlikely candidate for God's mercy. Joshua sends two spies into Shittim in preparation to overthrow the city. (Numbers 25:1-3 tells us that Shittim was where Israel took prostitutes and began Baal worship.) These two spies make it into the city and find their way to Rahab's house. The text does not tell us they went to her in order to have sex, but for some reason they are in her house. She risks her life and the life of her family by sheltering these spies. The Israelites eventually overthrow the city, destroying everything in it. But Rahab and all her family are saved, and they go to live with the Israelites.

Once again, we have to ask, why tell this story? Here's why. God takes a woman, one we may be tempted to turn our back on if she walked into our churches today, and he saves her and includes her in his master plan of redemption. Matthew 1:5-6 mentions "Salmon the father of Boaz by Rahab, and Boaz the father of Obed by Ruth, and Obed the father of Jesse, and Jesse the father of David the king."

Amazingly, neither Tamar nor Rahab were Israelites by birth, and both of them sold their bodies for sex, yet God was pleased to redeem these terrible situations and use the most unlikely of candidates to bring about his plan of redemption.

These amazing stories should reach down to the deepest fears we experience concerning our kids' sexuality. Regardless of atrocities that may happen to your children that are outside of their control, God can redeem them. Regardless of what your children decide to do sexually that is outside of your control, God can redeem them. There is no circumstance, there is no sin, there is no experience that can put your kids beyond his reach of grace. So turn to your Father with your fears. Turn to your Father with your children. Pray for grace to trust him. Pray for grace to believe in his love. Pray for grace to believe in his power to redeem.

These stories tell us we can trust God in the confusing, perplexing, unknowable, scandalous pits in our lives, resting in the knowledge that he is the great architect and that he will build exactly what he has said he will build. In your moments of unbelief, remember that he has forgiven you for all your lack of trust and given you his Son as a promise of his love. Remember that for every time you traded your body in order to feel loved, accepted, or wanted, you have been forgiven. Every time your body was used by others, your heavenly Father covered your shame.

Beloved, there is no sin, no circumstance, no family situation that will separate you from God's providential care. And if your situation is never resolved in a tangible way here on earth, know that one day all will be resolved. Tears will be a distant memory. Pain will never make an appearance again. Death will forever be dead. You and I will be with God, the lover of our soul, the rescuer we always longed for, and we will know complete happiness forever.

> There is no sin, no circumstance, no family situation
> that will separate you from God's providential care.

How does this sit with you? Do you wonder if God can or will include you in his plans? Let these stories encourage you.

Words for Dads

These stories highlight a few things we dads need to remember. First, God can enlist us in his plans regardless of where we are in our walk with Christ. God uses broken people to pour grace into other broken people. He can and will work through you, just as he worked through the people in these biblical accounts. He uses people like you and me to build his kingdom.

Second, as dads we have an incredible opportunity to talk to our sons about how to love women. We can demonstrate the truth in our actions. Women are not things to be used for our pleasure, but are human beings who are loved and cherished by God. We have the opportunity to show our boys and talk to our girls about the value of the opposite sex and how to treat them with respect and love.

So may I ask…do the words "respect" and "honor" describe the way you treat the women in your life? Is that how you talk about them? If so, then praise God! That is a clear evidence of God's work in your heart. If not, would you take the time to ask for forgiveness from God and from the women in your life? Would you humble yourself in front of them, showing how much you love them, because Christ humbled himself for you?

And would you start now to talk to your sons and daughters about things like sex trafficking, prostitution, and rape? Would you start to take a stand in your family and in the society around you against these injustices? So many of the people caught in these lifestyles are victims of incredible violence, and so often they have no voice. Would you and your teens start to become their voice?

Finally, tell your kids that sexual sin can be forgiven. As we have seen in these accounts, sexual sin is not the unforgivable sin. Augustine, a great father of the church, had a prostitute in his employ until he became a Christian. David committed adultery with Bathsheba. And a prostitute washed Jesus's feet! When your children commit sexual sin, treat it like what it is—a grave sin. But assure them of the forgiveness they have in Christ. If Christ can forgive you, me, Augustine, David, and the prostitute, he can and will forgive your children. Don't ostracize them; don't treat them as if they are dirty and ruined for life. Instead, promise to forgive them and love them and help them.[2] Help them be reconciled with Christ and others, and in the dark times when they are reminded of their sin, be the first one to remind them of the mercy they have in Christ.

Words for Moms

Sister, are you convinced that God can and does use any type of sexual history to bring about his good plan? Are you overwhelmed by shame because of your sexual past? Do you feel as if that is something you could never tell your children about? Do you think if they truly knew you, they wouldn't respect you or they would feel as if they could do whatever they wanted?

Or are you convinced of your own goodness? Do you look down on your husband, others, or even your children because of their sexual history?

If you have had any of those thoughts, this chapter is for you. We must see the deep brokenness of our sexuality. No one is born pure. You don't keep your purity until you are married. We are all born serving ourselves, looking to please ourselves, and using others to accomplish that goal. You may have been a virgin when you got married, but that doesn't mean that all your thoughts were sexually pure. (My guess is they weren't.) Even if you didn't really think about sex a whole lot and didn't engage in sexual activity, if there is any self-righteousness in your heart about those facts, you are just as in need of grace as the girl who was sexually active.

We need to build a culture of grace in our homes. Let your kids know that everyone is equally desperate for the saving grace of Christ. If your children have had issues with pornography, stand next to them with your arm around them and tell them you understand struggling with the same sin over and over again. Even the apostle Paul spoke about doing the very things he didn't want to do (Romans 7). Now, wisdom dictates taking other steps to help your children with their sexual sins besides just telling them you get it. But in the middle of the discipline and the help, make sure they don't view you as a superhero who has it all together. Make sure they know you are a sinner too. You could even show them these stories from the Bible and explain that sexually broken people are included in Jesus's genealogy. He doesn't exclude on the basis of the severity of the sin.

If our kids believe sexual sin is the worst sin they could commit, they will be ashamed to admit their failures and will try to hide them. They will seek comfort in the very act they know is destructive and wrong. Make a habit of confessing all sorts of sins to your children so they know they are safe to do the same with you.

Let your children know the dangers of pornography. Not only that it is dangerous for them and that studies have shown it physically alters the brain, but also that it is dangerous for the people in the pictures.[3] Frequently, those in pornographic videos and pictures are sex slaves, addicts, or people who believe they have no other choice. And Mom, you need to talk to your daughters about porn too. This isn't just a problem for boys. It is becoming more and more rampant among both sexes.

But our overriding theme in every conversation is that sexual purity doesn't make God love you more, and sexual impurity doesn't make God love you less. You are loved completely and wholly because of what Christ has done on your behalf. We must tell our kids that their only hope is that they are hidden in Christ, that he is the one who forgives prostitutes and pimps by his great redeeming love.

TALKING POINTS

- Each one of us is sexually broken.

- God uses sexually broken people to bring about his plan of redemption.

- Our sexual past never disqualifies us from grace. God's grace reaches each of us.

3

The Wisdom of Sexual Fidelity
When Sex Helps

How beautiful is your love, my sister, my bride!
How much better is your love than wine, and
the fragrance of your oils than any spice!
SONG OF SOLOMON 4:10

Jim was sitting in a service at our church, just as he had every Sunday for the past ten years. Next to him was his wife, Carrol—a beautiful woman who was totally committed to him. When she married Jim, she knew that he struggled with watching porn. What she didn't know was that Jim watched porn every night. She convinced herself that if he kept his porn watching to a minimum, she could live with it. But now it had gotten out of control—his addiction to porn had increased.

Carrol was pregnant, but Jim was spending more time at work and growing distant from her. She felt frustrated, ashamed, and insecure.

As the church service unfolded, we came to the point in the liturgy where we confess our sins and hear God's forgiveness. Somehow the message finally penetrated Jim's heart, and he heard as if for the first time that even though he had sinned terribly, he was forgiven because of Christ's work for him. He felt a freedom he hadn't known as an adult.

Jim and Carrol invited me (Joel) over to their house. We sat in their living room and cried together. We talked about Christ, about love, about what it means to forgive. Carrol decided in her heart that even though she had proper grounds to divorce Jim, she would not. She would work on their marriage.

Jim and I met every week for the next five months. We learned about the wisdom of how God designed sex and how pornography tears at the fabric of that beauty. We talked about how sex would never fully satisfy his deepest needs and desires. As we talked, we saw what the Bible had to say about the goodness of sex and how wisdom helps to guide our sexual activity. Jim and Carrol have had some bumps in the road, but it has been four years since we met last, and God has helped them experience healing in their marriage.

In the first two chapters we have seen that God created sex and that he made it very good, but sex was broken after the fall. Adam and Eve were naked and unashamed in the Garden, but after the fall, sex was used for power and selfish gain, rape infested our world, and people were sold for sex as if they were objects intended for the pleasure of others. But God redeems broken people and works through the least likely to build his kingdom. No one is so broken sexually that God cannot save, redeem, and include them in his great plan.

In this chapter, we would like to continue exploring God's plan for sex. We will expand on the idea that sex is a good thing and that there is wisdom in engaging in sexual activity. We want to show you from Scripture that even though everyone is sexually broken by the fall, God still wants us to have and enjoy lots of sex.

Now, as a man, I (Joel) get the side-eye every time I say this. I have preached on these chapters as well as the topic of sex nine times in the past five years, taught a high school Sunday school class on the topic, and talked at a conference about it. Every time I say God wants us to have and enjoy lots of sex, those of the fairer sex think I am up to something. But hold on...let us present you with the biblical evidence, and then you can decide.

Four books of the Bible will help us in this discussion: Proverbs, Ecclesiastes, Song of Solomon, and 1 Corinthians.

A Proverbial Sex Life

Let her breasts fill you at all times with delight;
be intoxicated always in her love.

PROVERBS 5:19

The book of Proverbs is written in an established tradition of wisdom literature. Its sayings are not meant to be taken as promises but as maxims for wise living, and we are meant to slow down and ponder their meaning. They are written by a sage and not a prophet, so rather than reading "Repent!" you will find "Consider."[1] Here is an example: "Go to the ant...consider her ways" (Proverbs 6:6). What is the point? Go look at an anthill for a while. The sage did, and he derived something good about God's creation and how we were made for work.

In Proverbs 5–7 we get to listen in on a discussion that a father has with his son about the goodness of sex within the confines of marriage. He contrasts that with the wiles of the prostitute. The father uses vivid images that are meant to stir up our imaginations. He uses everyday items from the natural world—honey, oil, wormwood, swords, cisterns, wells, fountains. All these images (and this is just in chapter 5) are meant to make the son stop and think about their characteristics.[2] Why don't you stop now, put this book down, and spend the next few minutes reading Proverbs 5–7. Write down your observations on the text. Then come back, and let's compare notes.

These three chapters provide a comprehensive guide for talking to children about the wisdom of sex in marriage as opposed to the folly of premarital or extramarital sex. In chapter 5, the main metaphor is taste. In chapter 6, it's fire, and in chapter 7, the father loses the metaphors altogether and describes the temptation itself. In all three chapters, the son is reminded of the goodness of his parents' teaching and instruction because they keep the son's heart and ways pure. In all three, the way of the temptress leads to short-lived pleasure and ultimate death.[3]

So if we are trying to lift up the beauty and goodness of sex, how is this helpful?

In chapter 5, the answer is in the metaphor. I (Joel) am a huge fan of chocolate, especially dark chocolate. When I eat a little, it is good...but then I go back for more. I eventually eat the entire bar, and that which at first tasted good ends up bitter and giving me a stomachache. This is the point. Sex outside the God-given confines seems great at first, but the problem is that connections are made during the act of sex that no relationship outside of the commitment of marriage can handle, and eventually it turns bitter and brings pain.

On the other hand, sex in marriage is like a refreshing glass of water that doesn't turn bitter in the end. And the father tells his son, enjoy it (verse 19)! Enjoy the pleasure of your spouse's body; it is not shameful! In fact, enjoy it so much that you are intoxicated—captivated, exhilarated, ravished, and staggering—with her love. The same word is used in the very next verse: "Why should you be intoxicated, my son, with a forbidden woman?" The point is that if sex in marriage can be that good, good enough to make you stagger as if you were intoxicated, why do that in a context that will only bring you pain? The answer is obvious! Don't! Instead, get your fill of marital sex!

> Sex in marriage is like a refreshing glass of
> water that doesn't turn bitter in the end.

Our culture has lied to us and to our children about this very thing. We hear that the way to be intoxicated by sex, the way to be sexually fulfilled, is to have various partners without true and lasting commitment. We hear that we should experiment and see what satisfies us the most. But the culture's lies will bring only pain, heartache, and harmful consequences. We must fight in our own hearts and fight for the hearts of our kids to lay hold of the truth that God's good plan for sex is the best plan for sex.

There are some people for whom sexual activity brings about either physical pain or emotional pain. Husbands and wives must take this into account, and parents should mention it when talking to their kids. Sex isn't all fun for all people. Some have been molested or raped, and some have anatomical issues. We need to learn to live with one another in an understanding way. There is much to be said about this, but we will not take the time to do that here. If sexual activity is a painful experience for you, please seek counseling. Open up that part of your life to a trusted individual who may be able to help you.

Now let's turn to the discussion of sex in Proverbs 6. Verses 20-21 read, "My son, keep your father's commandment, and forsake not your mother's teaching. Bind them on your heart always; tie them around your neck." We read the same sort of formula that we read in Proverbs 1, where the writer extols the value of wisdom. He then moves the discussion to hiring a prostitute and sleeping with a neighbor's wife. He says both are enticing and seem to be easily hidden. But notice that the price of a prostitute is "only a loaf of bread," whereas a married woman "hunts down a precious life" (verse 26). Either way it costs you, but one is far more destructive than the other. Then the writer uses the age-old saying that if you play with fire, you are going to get burned: "Can a man carry fire next to his chest and his clothes not be burned?" (verse 27). The implied answer is NO!

Even a thief can repay what he has stolen, but a man who has an affair with another man's wife accumulates a debt he can never repay. He takes something that can never be restored. Now this passage is hard to read, especially if you are someone who has had an affair before, and we need to take this warning very seriously. We need to warn our children about the reality of stealing another person's spouse sexually. But we also need to remind ourselves and our children that having an affair is not the unforgivable sin. But instead of playing with fire, it is best to do whatever we can to avoid it. Follow Joseph's example: When a married person approaches you, pray for strength to not give in and then run for your life!

We have seen that in the Sermon on the Mount, Jesus takes this deeper by saying that when we lust after a woman, we have committed adultery with her (Matthew 5:28). So what do we do? Do we give up and start having sex with every woman we meet because we are guilty? No! When we fall, we run to Christ, confess our sin to him, trust in his promise to forgive our sin, and then get up and try again. This is the pattern of the Christian life.

When we fall, we run to Christ, confess
our sin to him, trust in his promise to forgive
our sin, and then get up and try again.

Finally, consider Proverbs 7, the last of these three chapters on sex and the wisdom of sexual fidelity. The chapter is much like the one before it. It talks about a young man who is obviously sexually aroused and is lacking sense. He goes into the red-light district and is looking for a woman to have sex with. He allows lust to grow in his heart and goes out to fulfill his desires. And the woman meets him in the street.

In the past, this passage has been used to blame sexual sin on women, but honestly, the person looking could be a woman and the person waiting could just as easily be a man.[4] She talks seductively to him, and he gives in to his desires. He has already committed himself to this adulterous encounter. The writer of Proverbs says that this is the way to death, to Sheol. He says that the man may think he is her only lover, but she has had a "great throng" of victims. So instead the son ought to avoid her ways. This is particularly instructive for us because it is literally a conversation between parent and child about the pain and folly of sex outside of marriage.

You might be rolling your eyes right now because sex at home isn't that good, and you wish you hadn't waited to have sex. Or maybe you feel a distance from your spouse or possibly no sexual desire at all. These are not reasons to go outside of marriage to have sex, as that will only bring more pain and separation. Our prayer is that our next words will challenge and inspire you to find pleasure in your spouse.

The Vanity of Pleasure

I got...many concubines, the delight of the sons of man...
All was vanity and a striving after wind, and there was
nothing to be gained under the sun.
Ecclesiastes 2:8,11

The wisdom literature, particularly the book of Ecclesiastes, doesn't get much play in our pulpits. We learn from either Moses, Jesus, or Paul but rarely from the sage. We want fast answers, given on our time-table, but the sage doesn't play by our rules. We want instant gratifica-tion, but the sage won't budge. In the book of Ecclesiastes, the Preacher is wrestling with trying to find meaning in life, but all he finds is vanity or futility because nothing provides lasting satisfaction.

In our culture we want to elevate sex and make it more than it is—not just something to bring us pleasure, but the thing that makes us human. We, like the Preacher in Ecclesiastes, are looking for the mean-ing of life. Expressing your sexuality has become one of the forerunners in finding that meaning. The message from the world is clear: "Find out who you are sexually. Explore that to the fullest. You will find happi-ness and meaning. You will be your truest you." According to this line of thinking, our humanness rests on our ability to express ourselves sexually.

The Preacher brings us a bit of a counterweight. He says, "I got… many concubines, the delight of the sons of man." But unfortunately, "all was vanity and a striving after wind, and there was nothing to be gained under the sun." The Preacher chronicles his attempts at finding lasting meaning through an overuse of the good things of the world. He says, "I searched with my heart how to cheer my body with wine—my heart still guiding me with wisdom—and how to lay hold on folly, till I might see what was good for the children of man to do under heaven during the few days of their life" (verse 3). So along with build-ing gardens, having a well-run household, acquiring great possessions, and so on, he has sex. Lots of it.

There is a strong tradition that identifies Solomon as the Preacher. If that is the case (and I think it is), then he took this pursuit very seri-ously. He had 700 wives and 300 concubines (1 Kings 11:3).

After surveying his sexual conquests, there is no question that Sol-omon experienced the goodness of sex, but his misuse and overvalu-ing of sexual pleasure led him to the conclusion that it was vanity, or trying to catch the wind. Here we see the typical inflation of the value of sex, which actually leads to its deflation. That's what Solomon did then, and we do the same thing now. I think it is helpful for us to think about how this applies to us.

As we have seen, Jesus said that when we lust after another person in our heart, we have committed adultery with them. Now, I don't think anyone on my street in suburban San Diego is hiding 699 wives and 300 concubines. But when we look to pornography or extramarital sex, we are grasping after the same fulfillment Solomon did. Sex is good, but it cannot provide lasting fulfillment. Only Christ does.

Sex is good, but it cannot provide lasting
fulfillment. Only Christ does.

Proper imbibing of the goodness of sex keeps us from elevating sex to a Solomonic level, and it brings us pleasure without determining our identity. This means more than simply having sex with your spouse frequently. It includes employing your heart, soul, and mind. Awakening all your senses.

One common misconception about marriage is that if a couple is having sex regularly, things are good in the relationship. Sexual health is sometimes a marker of a good marriage, but not always. Often, when we find out that one spouse has had an affair, we wonder, *How often were the married couple having sex?* The truth of the matter is, Solomon wasn't satisfied with having sex every day—possibly multiple times a day with different women.

We are truly satisfied only when our hearts are first satisfied in Christ's love for us. Sex is meant to bring pleasure, but only the love of Christ brings identity. When we forget about the love of Christ or when we look to sex to define who we are, we will end up distorting it. We will use it in ways that it was not meant to be used.

We are truly satisfied only when our hearts are first
satisfied in Christ's love for us. Sex is meant to bring
pleasure, but only the love of Christ brings identity.

Our children will be tempted to use sex to define themselves, just as we are. At times, we even play into this temptation. We infer that if they aren't sexually active, they are somehow better than others who are. We teach them that their sexual goodness defines their identity. When we do that, we unintentionally teach them that failing sexually determines their identity as well. But when we find our satisfaction in Christ, the futile or vanity-filled search for identity through sexuality is cut off at the pass. Our sexual goodness, our sexual badness, our sexual desires…none of that is meant to reveal our true identity. None of it can bear the weight of sustaining our humanness. Only the truth that we are image bearers who have been loved and redeemed can sustain us in the search for meaning.

The Book of Love

> *I am my beloved's and my beloved is mine.*
> Song of Solomon 6:3

"Don't read this book until you are married."

"Single men should not read this book."

"Teens should not study this book—its content is too graphic and explicit."

All of this has been said about the Song of Solomon. The monastery, the small church, or the rabbinical school may warn that the Song is too hot to handle. It is full of euphemisms, double entendres, and word pictures that we are thankful remain as word pictures and don't get made into real pictures.

This part of this book is a little different from the others because the Song of Solomon is full of references to the goodness of sex in the context of marriage. So rather than focusing on one verse, we will read the entire book through the lens of this one verse.

But how do we read it? Is it purely a love story? Is it a picture of God's love for his people? This has been hotly debated over the centuries, but let me commend to you what Iain Duguid calls "combining natural and spiritual interpretation."

As wisdom literature, the Song is designed to show us an

idealized picture of married love, in the context of a fallen and broken world. As it does so, it intends to convict each of us of how far short of this perfection we fall, both as humans and as lovers, and thus to drive us repeatedly into the arms of our true heavenly husband Jesus Christ. He is the only One whose love for his bride is complete and perfect, and whose perfect love is our only hope in life and death.[5]

When we read these verses, we are meant to think of married love in all its fullness. They are not meant for us to read based solely on sex or purely as emotional love, but as the love that is expressed in the two becoming one. But ultimately, as we see how short we fall in the realm of loving and serving our spouse sexually, we are meant to think of Jesus. We are to be enraptured by his forgiveness extended to the sexually impure, the sexually broken. We are to know that we are loved, and we are to delight in that love. His love for his spouse, Jesus's love for the church, is the love that matters most in our lives.

Once we embrace that love, we are to give ourselves fully to each other and delight in the love that is found in the context of marriage. Sex is not bad, sex is not dirty, sex does not make you bad or dirty...sin does that. When we have sex and we delight in our beloved, we are participating in something much bigger than just the physical act. We are, in some way, showing off the love of Christ for his bride. We explore this topic in more detail in the next chapter. This is so much more powerful than a commitment to chastity because it reaches the sinner and the saint. (Of course, when you consider Jesus's words in Matthew 5:28, there really is just sinner.) Jesus loves to take a broken bride for himself, delight in her, and make her whole again.

Prostitutes, Sex, and Celibacy

Do not deprive one another, except perhaps by agreement for a limited time, that you may devote yourselves to prayer; but then come together again, so that Satan may not tempt you because of your lack of self-control.

1 CORINTHIANS 7:5

The apostle Paul was celibate—let's just get that out of the way here. He, like every other man, thought about sex, and we get a window into his thoughts in the letters to the Corinthian church. In 1 Corinthians 5–7, he builds a sexual ethic for a church living in a society much like American society today. These were real people who were struggling with real problems, such as division in the church, celebrity pastors, what a church service should look like, and suffering in the church. But they were also a church full of people who struggled to find the proper place for sexuality in their lives, and they wondered whether the church could or should have anything to say about it.

This church was kind of a mess. In chapter 5, a man is sleeping with his stepmother. The entire church knows about it, and they are okay with it because the man has power in the church. In chapter 6 we read about people in the church going to prostitutes. In chapter 7 we read about husbands and wives depriving each other. Let's take a look at each of these cases individually to see how the gospel and the church have an effect on our sexual activity.

Unloving Tolerance Versus Loving Your Neighbor

If I give away all I have, and if I deliver up my body to be burned, but have not love, I gain nothing.

1 Corinthians 13:3

In 1 Corinthians 5, we read of a case study on church discipline, and what does the apostle Paul bring up? Inappropriate sexual activity. A man is having sex with his stepmother, and Paul says, "Even the pagans don't do that!" He says that instead of being stoked about their tolerance, the Corinthians should mourn that they allowed this to go on.

Sexual immorality has an impact on the church. The gospel changes the way we view not only each other but also the way we act sexually. Tolerance of gross immorality is not a good thing, whereas discipline for the sake of restoration (the salvation of the soul) displays God's love.

Not much has changed since biblical times. In fact, in the area of tolerance, it has only gotten much worse. We are belittled and told we are small minded if we don't tolerate everyone's sexual expressions. We are not advocating shaming or belittling someone for their sexual expressions, but we are called to stand up for what is right. You don't have to agree with someone in order to love them. Rather than compromising our beliefs, we can disagree in a loving way. Tolerance of sin is not loving, especially if we see that what we are tolerating in someone's life will end up hurting them.

On the other hand, the church, in its desire to follow biblical commands, has forgotten that without love we are nothing. Paul emphasizes this in the same letter:

> If I speak in the tongues of men and of angels, but have not love, I am a noisy gong or a clanging cymbal. And if I have prophetic powers, and understand all mysteries and all knowledge, and if I have all faith, so as to remove mountains, but have not love, I am nothing. If I give away all I have, and if I deliver up my body to be burned, but have not love, I gain nothing (1 Corinthians 13:1-3).

We are told that having love is more important than having the most eloquent argument, knowing the right answers, possessing an incredible faith, and giving away everything we own. We must love while disagreeing. This is a painful and difficult directive, but we must attempt to follow it. Loving someone you disagree with includes having a relationship with them. This is more than a call to love—it is a call to have all sorts of people in your life, even people whose sexual ethics are different from yours.

> We must teach them the unchanging truth, but we must also teach them that we can love those who disagree with us.

We need to teach our children these truths. How do you talk in your home about people with differing sexual views? Do you belittle them?

Or do you honor them as image bearers who are broken? Our kids can see the hypocrisy in being judgmental and graceless. The model of tolerating others is so much more appealing to them, especially if they are struggling sexually. The model of judging others is appealing to them if they are being sexually pure. We must teach them the unchanging truth, but we must also teach them that we can love those who disagree with us.

Belonging to Each Other

In the latter half of chapter 6, Paul directly links our sexuality to our union with Christ.

> He who is joined to the Lord becomes one spirit with him. Flee from sexual immorality. Every other sin a person commits is outside the body, but the sexually immoral person sins against his own body. Or do you not know that your body is a temple of the Holy Spirit within you, whom you have from God? You are not your own, for you were bought with a price. So glorify God in your body (verses 17-20).

Does this make you feel uncomfortable? By now we should be coming to the conclusion that our sexuality is directly linked to the gospel, and that should make a difference in our lives.

Our sexuality is directly linked to the gospel, and that should make a difference in our lives.

In verses 12-14, Paul draws on the created order to make the link for us. He says that when we eat food, we are doing what our bodies are made to do. In the same way, our bodies are meant for sexual activity in the context of marriage, but when we use our bodies outside of that context to have sex, we are using our bodies improperly. Next comes the really uncomfortable part.

> Do you not know that your bodies are members of Christ? Shall I then take the members of Christ and make them

members of a prostitute? Never! Or do you not know that he who is joined [or holds fast] to a prostitute becomes one body with her? For, as it is written, "The two will become one flesh" (verses 15-16).

In essence what Paul is saying is that when we become Christians, our bodies are no longer ours alone. They are God's. Not only that, but they are temples of the Holy Spirit. But notice that Paul does not say, "So don't have sex." He doesn't put any limits on sex inside the proper confines of marriage. This is an especially important point to consider. When we use our bodies to sin sexually, we need to ask ourselves, *Whose body am I using?* The answer is, it belongs to Jesus.

The Sexually Wise Life

So, what do we do? Chapter 7 helps us. Paul commends two life-styles as wise sexually—marriage and celibacy.

Because of the temptation to sexual immorality, each man should have his own wife and each woman her own husband. The husband should give to his wife her conjugal rights, and likewise the wife to her husband. For the wife does not have authority over her own body, but the husband does. Likewise the husband does not have authority over his own body, but the wife does. Do not deprive one another, except perhaps by agreement for a limited time, that you may devote yourselves to prayer; but then come together again (verses 2-5).

This section of Scripture provides the basis for our understanding of sexual activity in marriage. We've looked at the creation mandate given in the Garden—to be fruitful and multiply. We also saw that the fall has broken us sexually, so now we use one another. But here Paul says that sex is meant to be used not for our pleasure only, but to serve one another. So the old order of sex being used as a weapon to control or manipulate is over. Instead, sex is used to bless the spouse, with each one seeking to serve and please the other.

Next, Paul says twice that he wishes his readers would be like him—single. Paul affirms not only the wisdom of sex but also the goodness of celibacy. Hear this clearly: Paul was celibate. Jesus was celibate. Singleness is not a gift that is given to the church, like healing or administration; it is an honored lifestyle. People who are celibate are not closeted homosexuals, and nothing is wrong with them. As a church, we have done a bad job holding out the goodness of singleness and celibacy. Paul says that if you are married, you should have enough sex to satisfy your spouse, and if you are not married, that is a good thing. In either case, live a life of service to others.

> Paul was celibate. Jesus was celibate. Singleness is not a gift that is given to the church, like healing or administration; it is an honored lifestyle.

Lauren Winner, in her excellent book *Real Sex*, says this about celibacy and the way God has designed sex for marriage:

> Our bodies and how we inhabit them point to the order of creation. God made us for sex within marriage; this is what the Reformed tradition would call a creational law. To see the biblical witness as an attempt to direct us to the created order, to God's rule of creation, is not to appeal to self-interest in a therapeutic or false way. It is rather to recognize the true goodness of God's creation; things as they were in the Garden of Eden are things at their most nourishing, they are things as they are meant to be. This is what Paul is saying when he speaks to the Corinthians: *Don't you know that when you give your body to a prostitute, you are uniting yourself to her?* To ask that question is to speak the wisdom of Proverbs in the idiom of law. It is a law that invites us into the created order of marital sex; a law that rightly orders our created desires for sexual pleasure and sexual connectedness; a law, in short, that cares for us and protects us, written by a Lawgiver who understands that

life outside of God's created intent destroys us. By con-
trast, life lived inside the contours of God's law humanizes
us and makes us beautiful. It makes us creatures living well
in the created order. It gives us the opportunity to become
who we are meant to be.[6]

Be what you are created to be. Be what God has created you to be.
This is our message to our kids.

Words for Dads

Dad, are these the categories you think in when you think about
sexual activity? Do you think sexual activity is about you and your
desires more than it is about service to your spouse? This is one of the
most important truths you can teach your sons. Sex is not primarily
about you. Sex is about the wisdom of loving your spouse. Wisdom is
known by her deeds; wisdom is known by the use of it. Even though
sexual activity is lauded as wise, it is not to be misused. Wisdom also
knows how and when to exercise restraint and self-control.

We need to stand against a culture that says sexual activity is all
about self-fulfillment. Our sons are constantly living for themselves—
their bodies are driving them toward that goal because their hormones
are going crazy. You can remember what that was like. Let me encourage you to take some time and think about how the writer of Proverbs
talks to his son. He doesn't hold back when upholding the beauty of
sex. He doesn't mince words. But he sets it in its proper context and
warns his son against making unwise decisions about sex.

Dad, it's time for us to have real, frank conversations with our teenage boys. We need to tell them, to instruct them. If we don't, they will
get their instruction from the producers of pornography or from their
friends. We need to ground our sons in the reality that sex won't fulfill all their desires. We need to ground them in the wisdom of loving
Christ and finding their satisfaction in him. We need to be honest and
tell them that when they seek satisfaction in lesser things, they will be
disappointed. When they take one of God's good gifts—sex—and use
it improperly, it won't satisfy their desires.

We need to tell them their bodies are created by God, in his image, and it is normal for them to feel the way they do. Their bodies are gifts from God, and they are to be used for the good of God's kingdom. There may come a day when that will include glorifying God in their bodies by having sex with their wives, or there may not. That is not for them to take hold of and decide. God isn't a cosmic killjoy. The Westminster Shorter Catechism proclaims, "Man's chief end is to glorify God and enjoy him forever."

Words for Moms

Married sister, I know you are tired. I know that when you have little ones, the thought of being touched by one more person in the evening when the kids are in bed can be overwhelming. But there is wisdom in having sex with your husband. It's not just to keep him close to home; it's not just to somehow ensure that he won't have a wandering eye. It is for you as well. The act of giving and receiving with your husband is good. It is the way God created us to relate. Naturally, there will be seasons when sexual intimacy is not as frequent, and that too is okay.

But please hear me: Your husband cannot fully satisfy your need for love and intimacy. Your truest, deepest longings will be fulfilled only by Christ.

Unmarried sister, you understand how difficult it is not to engage in sexual activity, and you probably miss the intimacy and pleasure of having sex. You are able to come alongside your kids in a unique way as you speak to them about the wisdom of sexual activity within the marriage covenant.

As we talk to our kids about sexual activity, we can once again proclaim the goodness of what God has created. We can confess how we have misused sex or others have used it for their sexual pleasure. We can affirm that even though we are sinners and we use things for our own gain, sexual activity according to God's design is still a good thing. We can tell our kids that the Bible talks about having sex, about sexual activity being fulfilling, and about creating intimacy. Build a biblical viewpoint for your children. Sex isn't dirty, so we don't have to hide it. We can be very up-front about the goodness of sex inside its proper boundaries and the potential dangers of it outside them.

Teach your children that the body is a good gift from God and that its desires are not bad. We must restrain our sexual desires, just as we do every other desire, but the restraint doesn't inhibit our happiness or pleasure. It enhances it.

As you share about the goodness of sex, make sure your kids know that the reason God confines it to the marital relationship is that God wants what is best for us. He wants us to be in covenant relationship with someone before we give ourselves fully to them. Sexual activity outside of marriage opens us up to heartache, and God wants to save us from that.

TALKING POINTS

Talking with your teen about the things we have discussed in this chapter can be difficult. Here are some talking points to help get the conversation going.

- God created our bodies to experience the pleasures of sexual activity. This reality can be freeing sexually in the right context but can also bring incredible pain when used out of the context of marriage.

- Sex is never about self-gratification. It is always about serving our spouse.

- Love guides wisdom. We love our kids and those whose views on sexuality differ from ours, and we speak to them out of that love, not out of a proud spirit.

- Our bodies are not our own—they are God's, and we are to

use them to serve our spouse by giving of ourselves sexually or by practicing self-control.

- Celibacy is a good thing. Our Lord was celibate. Sex does not make you more human, and marriage does not make you more valuable.

- Jesus loves broken people. Jesus forgives all our sins, including our misuse of sex.

4

Sex and the Consummation of the Kingdom of God

When Sex Is Fulfilled

Blessed are those who are invited to the marriage supper of the Lamb.

REVELATION 19:9

In chapters 1–3, we affirmed that we are sexual beings but that sex is not all we are—we are so much more. To put something like sex or sexuality at the core of who we are as humans is to miss the point of sex. Sex is a signpost of something so much better. We talked about how the Bible began with the marriage of Adam and Eve and ends with the marriage of Christ and the church. Our friend Sam Allberry says, "Human marriage, then, reflects the big story of the Bible—the big thing God is doing in the universe: making a people for his Son. And this story provides the key to understanding our sexuality."[1]

Christ and the church. Christ as the faithful, sacrificial husband, the church as the bride—though all too often like the unfaithful Gomer. Christ loving, serving, giving; the church receiving, chasing other lovers, returning at Christ's call. The church giving herself to things like buildings, politics, money, and fame. Trying to dress herself up in the sexy lingerie of the world to attract Christ as well as other lovers. Christ the faithful husband, without a wavering eye, always waiting and loving, never falling for any other bride.

Husband and wife—these are the terms God uses for Christ and the church. And the union we experience in the act of sex, the intimacy that it brings to our marriages, is a picture of our union with Christ and the intimacy we enjoy with him. Even the single person who is celibate is declaring with their life that they are waiting the union they will experience in the consummation of all things.

> Singleness, like marriage, has a unique way of testifying to the gospel of grace. Jesus said there will be no marriage in the new creation. In that respect we'll be like the angels, neither marrying nor being given in marriage (Matt. 22:30). We will have the reality; we will no longer need the signpost...We skip the appetizer, but we await the entrée.[2]

Sex and Fried Chicken

When I (Joel) think about the age to come, I don't think about sex. In fact, I feel a little bit odd writing a chapter about how the consummation of the kingdom plays a deep role in the way we think and act sexually. But we think it does. In fact, the more we talk about it to our friends, the more they agree: The union and joy we experience during sex is a faint picture of the joy we will experience when we are reunited to Christ at his return. How does that strike you? Does it make you feel odd? Uncomfortable? Does the thought of trying to explain this concept to your kids make you want the earth to open up and swallow you whole? If so, you're not alone. So let me explain.

First, I want us to start out with an analogy. I love to eat—maybe a bit too much. I especially love fried chicken and collard greens. Whenever they are around, I cannot get enough of them. The other day I visited a new fried chicken place here in San Diego named the Crack Shack. This restaurant is known for having the best fried chicken in San Diego, so my friend Rob asked me to meet him there. I was skeptical—I had eaten really good fried chicken before and doubted the goodness of the Crack Shack.

We ordered our chicken and sides and then took a seat next to the giant chicken mural. Rob and I were in a deep discussion about Harry Potter and how our kids tried to cast spells on members of the churches where we are pastors when the chicken was delivered. I grabbed a drumstick, took a bite, and was transported to a different realm, the realm of chicken goodness, where only the best-tasting chickens live. In fact, the chicken was so good, so flavorful, so moist and tender, I actually told Rob to stop talking because I was having a moment. I caught a glimpse of something so much better, something so much more beautiful than just a piece of fried chicken.

There have been times in my life when my wife, Ruth, and I have felt distant from each other. Perhaps I was being a jerk, or maybe I was being a jerk *and* we were both super busy with work. The feeling was palpable when I was in seminary and working two jobs. With a schedule like that, it was easy to just fall apart from each other. But whenever we went out on a date, got a really nice dinner, and engaged in wonderful conversation, we reunited and experienced joy, comfort, and peace. The reunion pointed us to something we are waiting for, and this gave us joy that was far beyond just a nice dinner and conversation.

Both of these stories reveal two truths about all of us: We long for something more than what we experience here on earth, and the pleasures of this earth (especially the really good ones) point us to an ultimate longing that is fulfilled only in Christ. Our mom, Elyse Fitzpatrick, says in her book *Home* that the little good things we experience here on earth expose our longing for the consummation of God's kingdom. C.S. Lewis refers to this in his classic work *Mere Christianity*.

> Creatures are not born with desires unless satisfaction for these desires exists. A baby feels hunger; well, there is such a thing as food. A duckling wants to swim; well, there is such a thing as water. Men feel sexual desire; well, there is such a thing as sex. If I find in myself a desire which no experience in this world can satisfy, the most probable explanation is that I was made for another world.[3]

Lewis is cluing us in on something that we all know to be true. The temporary pleasures we experience in life are good and point us to a greater, more satisfying pleasure that is found in Christ. So let me flesh this out a bit for us.

A Longing

But for Adam there was not found a helper fit for him.
Genesis 2:20

When God created humanity, he gave Adam and Eve to each other, and they lived with God in perfect harmony. This union with God and each other placed in the human heart a desire, a longing for God and for others. The fall has taken away that perfect harmony, but that does not mean the longing no longer exists. We just try to fulfill it in ways that can't and won't satisfy us. That is why so often people who don't feel love try to gain it by giving themselves sexually. The union we experience with one another when we have sex reflects a longing for union with our Creator.

> The union we experience with one another when we have sex reflects a longing for union with our Creator.

This reality once again shows us that sex is about so much more than just a physical reaction or procreation, more than us and our desires. Sex is about union, closeness, and desires longing to be fulfilled. In the Garden, Adam looked for a companion for himself but could not find one. His desire was unfulfilled. Genesis 2:20 says, "The man gave names to all livestock and to the birds of the heavens and to every beast of the field. But for Adam there was not found a helper fit for him." So, what does God do? He recognizes that desire and fulfills it with Eve.

> The Lord God caused a deep sleep to fall upon the man,
> and while he slept took one of his ribs and closed up its

place with flesh. And the rib that the LORD God had taken from the man he made into a woman and brought her to the man (Genesis 2:21-22).

God, after seeing the goodness of their union, pronounces creation "very good" (Genesis 1:31). They were naked, they were unashamed, they knew each other, and it was good.

God placed this longing for companionship and love, for emotional and sexual intimacy, at the very core of who we are right from the beginning—before Adam and Eve sinned. And it was good. This is an important point, and it bears explaining. The longing that Adam had for a helper suitable for him was not a sinful desire. In fact it was the only part of the creation process that needed to be finished. Adam's desire exposed the only thing in creation that God saw and called "not good" (Genesis 2:18). The union Adam experienced with Eve was not sinful. The sex they enjoyed was not sinful, and nothing was wrong with their desires to be fulfilled in one another. We all desire intimacy—not just sex, but a relationship with someone who truly understands who we are, who is a "helper fit" for us.

This longing, this desire, cannot find its ultimate fulfillment in the sexual act. It never could. Adam and Eve experienced ultimate fulfillment not in the act of sex, but in their relationship with each other, which was built on their relationship with God. I (Joel) grew up believing that sex would lead to me feeling loved. But after 17 years of marriage to a woman whom I love and who I know loves me, I can honestly tell you (and she would agree) that sex does not satisfy our hearts' desire to be chosen and accepted and loved. People will tell our kids that the way to be loved and to show love is to have sex. But sex is just part of the bigger picture. It cannot stand up to the pressure of meeting our deepest needs.

Jesus said, "Greater love has no one than this, that someone lay down his life for his friends. You are my friends" (John 15:13-14). Only one love can satisfy the longing built into us. Only one person can fulfill the desires of our hearts to be accepted, even with all our problems. Only one person can pull off the greatest act of love ever displayed, and that person is not me, my spouse, you, your child, your teen's crush, or any other mere human being. Your teen needs to hear this! This is the good news, that though they slap God in the face again and again by sinning sexually in thought, word, and deed, Jesus still loves them enough to satisfy their longing to be loved.

> Come, everyone who thirsts, come to the waters, and he who has no money, come, buy and eat! Come, buy wine and milk without money and without price. Why do you spend your money for that which is not bread, and your labor for that which does not satisfy? Listen diligently to me, and eat what is good, and delight yourselves in rich food. Incline your ear, and come to me; hear, that your soul may live; and I will make with you an everlasting covenant, my steadfast, sure love for David (Isaiah 55:1-3).

What is Isaiah talking about? Finding satisfaction in the only thing that will satisfy—the "rich food" of Christ. This rich food is the life-giving, everlasting covenant displayed in the steadfast, sure love that comes only from Christ. Sex is good, and it should enhance a couple's intimacy, but it never satisfies completely. How do we know that? Because even the most intimate and fulfilling sex leaves you desiring more.

Clearly, we don't feel completely satisfied all the time. So we go to things like sex to fulfill our longing. But the satisfaction we do feel is enough to remind us that there is more out there for us to experience. That complete satisfaction will come at the end of days, when Jesus returns and takes us home. Then we will be fully united to Christ, body and soul, and we will be satisfied. This is what sex awakens in us.

This is the good news, that though they slap God in the face again and again by sinning sexually in thought, word, and deed, Jesus still loves them enough to satisfy their longing to be loved.

A Picture

*This mystery is profound, and I am saying
that it refers to Christ and the church.*

EPHESIANS 5:32

To help us understand the relationship between the people of God and God himself, one of the pictures the Bible often uses is of marriage. The Old Testament prophets speak of God seeing his people and engaging them in marriage. Isaiah 54:5 says, "Your Maker is your husband, the LORD of hosts is his name; and the Holy One of Israel is your Redeemer, the God of the whole earth he is called."[4]

John the Baptist describes Jesus as a bridegroom and himself as the best man. "The one who has the bride is the bridegroom. The friend of the bridegroom, who stands and hears him, rejoices greatly at the bridegroom's voice. Therefore this joy of mine is now complete" (John 3:29).

The apostle Paul uses marriage as the closest analogy of the relationship between Christ and the church.

> Husbands, love your wives, as Christ loved the church and gave himself up for her, that he might sanctify her, having cleansed her by the washing of water with the word, so that he might present the church to himself in splendor, without spot or wrinkle or any such thing, that she might be holy and without blemish...This mystery is profound, and I am saying that it refers to Christ and the church (Ephesians 5:25-27,32).

In Revelation 19, the apostle John refers to the consummation of the kingdom as a marriage feast celebrating the union of Christ and the church. What does this mean? In some way, the connection we experience in marriage helps us understand the connection we will have with Christ in the renewal of all things.

The consummation of God's plan for creation will be like a marriage. The give-and-take we experience in the best times of our marriages, the living for one another's joy and love, the connection we enjoy sexually—these are pictures of the give-and-take, the joy and love, the connection we will experience at Christ's return.

You may long for that sort of marriage. You may have suffered abuse or divorce, or your spouse may be distant. Hear this: Jesus is your true and better husband. You're married to him already. Everything you wish your spouse would be or would have been, Jesus is to you. I know that is easy for me to write, but even in the best of marriages there are unfulfilled longings, unfulfilled desires. Sex is not just about our pleasure; it is a picture of the relationship we already have with Christ—a relationship we will experience more fully in the consummation of God's kingdom.

> Hear this: Jesus is your true and better husband. You're married to him already. Everything you wish your spouse would be or would have been, Jesus is to you.

Sex is not everything. Isn't that beautiful? A marriage is about so much more than sex. Humanity cannot be defined by sexuality. At Christ's return, we will experience a reunion, a more complete union, an abundance of self-giving love. Our sexuality here on earth is just a foretaste of that.

We must share this truth with our children. Marriage is more than finally being able to have sex. As anyone who has been married knows, people who go into marriage thinking the best part of marriage is sex will be disappointed.

The world will tell our kids that sex is everything. We can accidentally give kids the same misconception by describing sex as the end-all of marriage. Teaching your children about the deep complexity of marriage is a long, involved process, but it will reap a harvest of benefits. Showing your teens that intimacy includes much more than sex will help them understand the relational dynamics between Christ and the church.

There is a constant drive to make sex just about ourselves, to make sex the thing that defines us and yet can be had anytime with anyone. This selfish view of sex and sexuality mars the beautiful picture that sex is just one part of our identity and our relationship with each other. Our kids need this sort of image of sex, not the cheapened image of pornography, and not the selfish image of sexual identity. Sex is ultimately meant to remind us about Christ's relationship to the church! When our view of sex and sexuality is placed into this larger picture, we see both the importance of sex and where it fits into the grand scheme of things.

A Relationship

Christ loved the church and gave himself up for her...so that he might present the church to himself in splendor, without spot or wrinkle or any such thing, that she might be holy and without blemish.
Ephesians 5:25,27

Our sexuality points us to one part of the relationship we will have with Jesus in heaven. Until the 1960s, sex was not believed to be "casual" and appropriate with anyone, anytime, anywhere. Before then, sex was still considered valuable. In the sex act, we share a portion of ourselves that is valuable, and we want to share that only with someone we are able to trust. This is one of the reasons rape and molestation are so horrible. They are forceful acts of taking something the victim has not given the perpetrators permission to take. This is a terrible wrong and should never be inflicted on another human being.

When sex is shared in the context of marriage, it can deepen and strengthen the bond and the love that a husband and wife share. This deepening, this strengthening, is just a dim picture of the love, the "naked and unashamed" oneness we will experience with Christ when he makes all things new. On our best days as husbands and wives, we desire to give to our spouses the love they long for, and our spouses reciprocate in self-denying love. On those days we experience joy. We think to ourselves, *Boy, I wish every day could be like today.*

Marriage, sex, and union. These three, put together, do not describe the totality of marriage, but they do help us describe the richness of sexuality in marriage. Two people are joined as one spiritually, physically, and emotionally. So often though, the baggage we carry into our marriages can really mess things up. Think about how often people have been told that if they have sex before marriage, they are used, and no one will want them. When people have sex outside of marriage, either by their own choice or because of rape or molestation, the people drag this heavy weight with them. They ask themselves, *If my spouse finds out what happened, will they love me?* Sadly, sometimes the answer is no. The relationship is broken and lost.

But when we sit at the marriage feast, there will be no need to hide. Christ, our husband, already knows everything we have experienced, and he has already decided to love and accept and forgive his bride. He will sit clothed in his wedding garment, beautiful and clean (a metaphor of his holiness and purity), and we sit across from him with all our sins forgiven, all our brokenness healed, and feel the warmth of his loving gaze. We will touch his nail-scarred hands and be totally accepted in spite of our pasts. We know this to be true because it has already happened, and when we experience that reunion, it will be glorious.

This is the beauty of Christ.

An old sermon talks about "the expulsive power of a new affection."[5] In it, the pastor explains that when we love our sin (in this case, sexual sin), we need something much more beautiful, something we can love more than we love our sin. And when we begin to love that person more than our sin, we begin to sin less. The new affection expels (expulses) the old. This hopeful picture—of Christ loving us and accepting us in the face of our sin, even presenting to himself a spotless bride (Ephesians 5:27) to spend all eternity with in perfect union—has this sort of expulsive power.

Is this the picture of Christ you are presenting to your teen? Is this the picture of sexual purity you are giving to your teens? This is what our teens need to hear. There is fulfillment to be found in Christ.

Delayed Fulfillment

We live in a world that craves instant gratification. We think we need to do something to fulfill every urge. Our culture feeds off our impatience and lack of self-control. We are consistently told in Scripture that our ultimate fulfillment is found not in the pleasures of this world, but in the coming day of Christ's return. So we have a future hope that brings present fulfillment, not instant gratification. We teach our teens that their hope is not in the sex they can have today, but in the satisfaction they will have in the coming renewal of all things. Then we live the way we talk. We seek to show that the satisfaction found only in Christ is far superior to the counterfeit satisfaction found in sin. In short, we practice self-control.

This may sound like an odd thing to say in a chapter about the consummation of God's kingdom, but that is the point that so much of the New Testament makes. We don't live for instant gratification, but for the future hope of glory. We aren't motivated by the instant pleasure of this world, but by the coming weight of glory. And that glory motivates us to put off the desires of the flesh and live in the light of eternity.

Let's work this out practically. For some, the struggle with same-sex attraction is very real and very difficult. They live their lives with desires to be fulfilled in that way, and when they look at the opposite sex, they are not physically attracted. Both Ed Shaw and Wesley Hill have written beautifully about this struggle, and in both of their books they advocate for a form of self-control that seems so foreign and repressive for the modern world: celibacy. What can motivate them to choose celibacy as a way of life? Only the restoration of all things.

This is true for everyone, not just for people who struggle with same-sex attraction. The ultimate motivation to live a life of sexual self-control is the renewal of all things, the future hope that all our needs will be fulfilled in ways we cannot even imagine! The fulfillment of our gospel hope moves us to practice self-control.

The fulfillment of our gospel hope
moves us to practice self-control.

Yes, this is a countercultural mindset. That is the understatement of the year. But the culture is adrift, so we need to be countercultural. This has been the place of the church from its beginning. The church needs to regain its prophetic voice. Believers need to practice lives that don't give in to the instant gratification offered by this age.

I (Jessica) once heard Kathy Keller talk about how difficult it is to be celibate or wait for marriage before engaging in sexual activity. She then pointed us to Jesus, the one who has been saving himself for us. Our true bridegroom never engaged in sexual activity when he was a man. And he *was* a man, tempted just as we are, but he never gave in to sexual temptation because he was saving himself for the final restoration—for the day when he will give himself fully to us and we will give ourselves fully to him. And here is the really lovely part: Christ's perfect obedience in all sexual activity is now our record before a holy God. So we don't have to be ashamed. We are loved and accepted and forgiven right now, and one day we will be able to understand just how astonishing that truth is.

Words for Dads

Dad, what do you think about sex? How does that affect what you are saying to your kids? Have you ever thought about sex in these sorts of larger, eternal categories? How does this chapter confront your view of sex in this world? When you begin to take a long-term view of sex, your view of the goodness of God's creation grows. As God confronts our shallow views of sex and sexuality, he deepens our relationship with him and with our spouse.

I hope you would never think about cheating on Jesus, never desire to go and bow down before an idol and worship it (although we do those things all the time).[6] In the same way, because our marriage and sex reflect our union with Christ, I hope that cheating on your wife is unthinkable as well. Dad, when you look at porn, lust after other women, or don't protect your wife, you are acting contrary to your salvation.

The satisfaction Christ gives you is so much better than anything you can experience by going to a false idol.

The satisfaction Christ gives you is so much better than anything you can experience by going to a false idol. In the same way, the satisfaction you can enjoy in married sex is so much better than the empty feeling of chasing after sexual fantasies.

I hope these little "Words for Dads" have helped you see that the way you think about a topic affects the way you act and talk about it. If you understand sex as existing only for your pleasure, you will treat it lightly. You will talk about it flippantly. You will not display the beauty of the richness of the relationship we have in Christ.

Now you may be thinking, *Joel, stop lecturing me. You're all over my case! I can barely get up and read my Bible in the morning, let alone feel a richness in my spiritual life that would change who I am and how I view my life.*

Well, dear friend, Christ's love for you is not like your love for him. It isn't based on how you feel about him; it is based on his covenant love for you (see Isaiah 55:3). Let me encourage you to meditate on that. To meditate on the reality that his love for you never grows cold the way yours does for him. Here is the kicker—his love for you doesn't change because of what you give to him or provide for him.

When you are sexually distant from your wife, that is oftentimes an indicator of the closeness of your larger relationship with your wife. But the strength of your relationship with Christ is not based on you. You can praise God for that!

Is this how you understand your salvation? Do you see it as that good? Romans 6:1-14 puts this into clear relief. Paul explains the gospel (verses 1-10) and then tells the Roman believers to think about themselves differently (verse 11) and to let that thinking shape their actions (verses 12-14). Now do you see how important it is that you think a certain way? Capture your kids' imagination with this view of sex; give them this sort of understanding of sex. Then encourage them to act on this belief.

Words for Moms

What picture of sex are you holding out to your teens? What picture of sex are you rehearsing in your mind? Do you think of it as a coming together? Have you ever considered that it might point to something bigger, richer, deeper? We Christians understand that what we experience here on earth isn't our full reality. We were made for something more. So as we experience the goodness of sex here, we can know that sex is ultimately pointing to our union with Christ. As we experience the brokenness of sex here, we can know that there will come a day when we will know true healing.

Our sexual experiences here on earth aren't all there is. We were made for something more. We can share that truth with our kids by telling them about "the expulsive power of a new affection" (though maybe not in those terms), by affirming that the longing to be fully known and united to someone will ultimately be fulfilled in heaven. Tell your children that the love and affection they are longing for is found in Christ.

Construct a bigger, better picture of what sex is about. The world cheapens sex even while saying that a good orgasm is the most fulfilling thing in the universe. It makes it simultaneously too small and too big. The truth is, it is a big deal, but we look forward to something more, something better. Talk to your kids about heaven and build a longing in their hearts for the beauty and fulfillment that await them there. You will be able to do this only as you yourself cultivate a desire to finally be truly home with God.

TALKING POINTS

This chapter gives us another opportunity to talk with our kids about what sex is all about. It's so much more than merely an act—it is about our relationship with Christ. Here are some talking points to help get the conversation started.

- Our desire for sex reveals something more about our desire to be loved and accepted—a desire that can be fulfilled only in Christ.

- Jesus loves, accepts, and fulfills his people, and he will do that fully at the end of days.

- Sex is a picture of the ultimate union and reunion that will happen in the consummation of the kingdom of God.

- Celibacy is not a bad thing or a "less than" life.

- Sex will never be able to completely fulfill our desire for intimacy, love, and acceptance. But one day we all will experience that complete fulfillment when we are with him.

Part 2

Sex and Our Culture

5

Friend Goals
How Friendship Is Shaping Our Teens

The soul of Jonathan was knit to the soul of David,
and Jonathan loved him as his own soul.

1 SAMUEL 18:1

In chapter 4, we saw that our conversations with our teens about sex and sexuality will be most helpful when we place them in the context of our relationship with Christ—our longing for him, his unconditional acceptance of us, and the incredible future awaiting us. Now let's look at another helpful context for those conversations. Our teens are more likely to go into marriage with a healthy view of sex if they see marriage as a friendship.

The message our kids are hearing from society and even from their own hearts is very different from this. According to the culture, sex is primarily about physical attraction, about a sexual spark. With Tinder and other dating apps, you simply look at someone's picture to decide whether you want to hook up with them. One of the first questions asked when talking about someone of the opposite sex is, "Are they hot?" Sex has been reduced to a physical act, but of course, it is so much more than that.

This is nothing new. It has been going on from the beginning, and we see examples of it all over the Bible. I am sure King Xerxes wasn't looking to be friends with Esther (or his many other concubines) when he took her into his harem. David didn't think Bathsheba had a great personality when he forced her into his bedroom. When we focus on sexual attraction and physical appearance, we devalue the sexual act. You can try to ignore the intimacy that comes with having sex, but it will take its toll on you emotionally and sometimes physically.

Our job as parents is to show our teens that sex is more than physical attraction, more than having an intense orgasm. Sex is meant to be about the whole person—body, soul, and heart. Engaging every aspect of our being is what makes sex so beautiful. Cultivating this holistic view of sex will be a benefit to your kids because as we all know, our bodies get old, saggy, lumpy, and soft. When that happens, we need something deeper than sexual attraction to keep us committed in our marriages. We need lasting friendship. We need heart-level intimacy that keeps us attracted to our spouse. Friendship is an important but often overlooked component of marriage.

> We need lasting friendship. We need heart-level intimacy that keeps us attracted to our spouse.

Many people choose a marriage partner simply because the other person is sexy, and they overlook the intangible qualities that make for a good friend. The two never become good friends, and they find themselves stuck in a strained marriage. The sexual appeal isn't strong enough to bridge the distance between them. They feel frustrated, and the marriage lacks true love.

This is a common setup in TV shows and movies. A man marries a woman because both of them are beautiful, but within a few months, the man has wandering eyes. He meets a woman at work, they become friends, they notice they have shared interests and goals, and they commit adultery. The man realizes he never actually was friends with his wife. He either stays in the marriage and is unhappy, or he divorces her and we are all supposed to be happy for him.

Fortunately, we all know people who are married and are great friends. They may not like the same things, but they stick together and support each other. They look out for each other's interests and seek to serve each other. As the two grow old together, they may stop having sex, but they are happy to be with one another. Their friendship has grown so deep that sexuality is only one small part of who they are together as a couple.

This is totally unsexy in one sense. It's just ordinary. It's a radical departure from what we see in much of our society. Let's fight for this truth in our own marriages and in the lives of our kids.

The relational dynamics of building strong friendships are learned early. Children see and learn how healthy friendships are worked out in communities—at home, at school, in church, on sports teams, and so on. As they learn the rules of relationships, they follow some rules and break others. If we want our children to be in healthy relationships when they grow up, we must help them understand from an early age what those relationships look like.

The Rise of the Friend Group

I (Joel) am a youth and family pastor, and one of my favorite things is to watch the relational dynamics between kids at my small Southern California church. I love it when I see "my kids" reaching out and trying to be friends with one another. Kids run in packs, and relationships are formed in this pack mentality. Even the outsiders have their own groups.

I was introduced to the concept of the friend group while riding in the car with my daughter, who is a social butterfly like me. Some of her friends were with us, and as they were talking about their friendship, she said something about "friend group goals." I was confused. I know I'm old, but I'm not *that* old. I hang out with kids all the time. Trying to not lose social status, I kept my question to myself. Later I asked, "What's a friend group?"

She looked at me with those "Dad, you are such a dork!" eyes and said, "It's your group of friends." I guess I could have figured that out.

We all grew up with this pack mentality, and I can remember people being suspicious of my own friend group. We were a bunch of SoCal surfers who listened to punk rock and dyed our hair. We hung out all the time, we had each other's backs, we loved each other, we attended youth group together, we went to Mexico and surfed together, we got in trouble together. Sometimes a girl would try to invade our friend group, but most couldn't hang...that is, until our young male hormones kicked in. We talked about girls as a pack, we flirted with girls as a pack, we dated girls as a pack. We learned about relationships in a pack.

We thought we knew it all, but we didn't know anything. Still, this communal aspect of our friendships is so important. I look back at those days with fondness. (My daughter would probably think I was a dork for using the word "fondness.")

These friend groups are vital for understanding how to live in the new friend group that our kids will be growing into—a family.

Friendships and Relational Dynamics

There is a friend who sticks closer than a brother.
PROVERBS 18:24

Where do we learn how to function as a family? Primarily from our families of origin, but secondarily from our friend groups. We see how Dad and Mom treat each other relationally and physically. This helps us as we determine who we want to spend our lives with and how that relationship will work. But some key relational dynamics are developed in the friend group.

We men learn how to view women. We pick up on the social views of our friends, and that shapes our understanding of the relationships between men and women. We make friends with women and learn how they like to be treated, what makes them mad, and how to be there for a person of the opposite sex in a nonsexual way.

The problem arises when our sinful nature (our desires to control, use, and dominate) mix with bad nurture (poor family life, disrespectful friend group) to produce sinful desires in us. For Christian teens, there is no neutral ground. The world, the flesh, and the devil will always be warring against the Spirit's work inside them, and friends can provide a helpful check against those things that would draw them away to sin.

> The world, the flesh, and the devil will always be warring against the Spirit's work inside them, and friends can provide a helpful check against those things that would draw them away to sin.

Scripture reveals God's thoughts about friendship, how our friendships shape the way we act, and what sort of people we should surround ourselves with.

- "The righteous choose their friends carefully, but the way of the wicked leads them astray" (Proverbs 12:26 NIV).

- "One who has unreliable friends soon comes to ruin, but there is a friend who sticks closer than a brother" (Proverbs 18:24 NIV).

- "Two are better than one, because they have a good return for their labor: If either of them falls down, one can help the other up. But pity anyone who falls and has no one to help them up. Also, if two lie down together, they will keep warm. But how can one keep warm alone? Though one may be overpowered, two can defend themselves. A cord of three strands is not quickly broken" (Ecclesiastes 4:9-12 NIV).

- "Do not be misled: 'Bad company corrupts good character'" (1 Corinthians 15:33 NIV).

These four Scripture passages represent so much of what God has to say on this matter. Be careful who your friends are.

Now, we must be careful when talking about a subject like this in this way. Scripture is meant to be read as a guide to proper, God-honoring living, but as we will see in a minute, Jesus surrounded himself with people who were outcasts. We are not called to live in a monastery and separate ourselves from unbelievers, but those whom we trust with our hearts need to share a common goal—glorifying God.

Understanding these truths from Scripture and helping our kids understand them while still engaging the culture can be tough. It is difficult to know how to let your kids be a part of the culture and let them have friends without letting fear rule in our hearts. The desire to completely control who your kids are friends with is strong. We do this for a number of reasons. We might be fearful that the friends are a bad influence. We might not like the way they treat our children. We might just have automatic biases based on the way the friends look or talk.

But we cannot let our own fears rule how we communicate with our kids about their friends. If you have a specific concern about a friend, ask your child questions about that kid. You might be completely misinformed. Don't just assume you know everything about the situation. I (Jess) have also found that if I don't particularly like one of my kids' friends, inviting that child into our house and sharing a meal or taking them somewhere fun is a great way to get to know them and possibly change my opinion of them.

Ultimately though, if your child has a friend whom you believe to be detrimental to your child, you will have to place boundaries on that friendship. That is something you will need to do with grace and kindness and lots of prayer.

As your kids get older, they will be making their own decisions about friends. It would behoove us to try our hardest not to exclude or cut off friendships for our kids. I know there are times when this must happen, but generally it is better to be inclusive and inviting than it is to regulate all of your children's relationships. We cannot control this area of their lives forever, and at some point you have to trust God with the decisions your kids make in this area.

Can We Just Be Friends?

Here is where things get sticky. When I (Joel) was growing up, I had both male and female friends. Both groups taught me so much about how to be a good friend. But I have to admit, when I grew close to a female friend, it was sometimes difficult to separate my love for them as a friend from my feelings of attraction. I have had to learn how to be affectionate with people of either sex without being sexual.

This an important aspect of our conversations with our teens. Friendship and affection are not the same thing as sexual attraction. Having friends of the opposite sex deepens our ability to relate to others, increases our understanding of issues they face, and prepares us for future relationships.

This helps us become fuller human beings, it teaches us self-control, and it helps us decouple sexual attraction from affection. This is one aberration in American culture—affection is tied too closely to sex. Simple signs of affection shown between friends don't have to be sexual, but bodily contact between teens is usually couched in those terms. Why? Because as a culture, we seem to be losing the ability to distinguish between affection and sexual attraction.

Attraction

This is one of the most important topics you can talk to your teens about. The world is telling them all the time how to react to attraction—by having sex. Our teens' hormones tell them to have sex. Even our teens' friends tell them to have sex. The question then becomes, what do you say? How do we talk to our kids about the feelings they have for a teen of the opposite sex? A few things come to mind.

Fulfillment

*Whoever drinks of the water that I will give
him will never be thirsty again.*
JOHN 4:14

First, assure them that sex will not fulfill them. When our kids think about their lives, they want to feel fulfilled, they want to be satisfied. This desire is something that has been in us since the Garden. They want to satisfy the urge building within them for love, intimacy, and sexual pleasure. What they are missing is the maturity and life experience that helps them understand that sex will not fulfill that. That is where you come in. You get the opportunity to talk with them and to show them that sex will not ultimately satisfy them.

> You get the opportunity to talk with them and to show them that sex will not ultimately satisfy them.

Talk with your kids about the woman at the well, who was seeking satisfaction but never could find it—even though she'd had multiple partners—until she met the living water who satisfies (John 4). Tell them about your own experience. Yes, it is awkward at first, but open and honest conversations like these help them place their world in the proper context. Throughout the Old Testament we read the command, the wisdom, for parents to talk to their children about all of life. Use this open door to speak the words of the gospel into their lives. These conversations build bridges that you and your teen can walk back and forth on throughout your lives together.

True Beauty

Second, help them to understand attraction and true beauty. Our culture pushes the agenda that a woman has to be thin and have the six-pack of a body builder (and strangely, no cellulite), huge breasts, and a big butt. How this happens naturally I don't know, but this is the standard for women. Men have to have the body of Adonis and the disposition of your daughter's BFF. They must be hairless, have no pudge, and be able to both dance and not care about dancing. And in two or three years, this description will be outdated.

> Beauty is more than just flat abs, huge breasts, and
> legs of granite. This is basic stuff, but we have to talk
> to our kids about it because they live in a voyeuristic
> age where beauty is judged by a picture.

Is there something wrong with physical beauty? No. But beauty is more than just flat abs, huge breasts, and legs of granite. This is basic stuff, but we have to talk to our kids about it because they live in a voyeuristic age where beauty is judged by a picture. First Peter 3:3-4 says,

> Do not let your adorning be external—the braiding of hair and the putting on of gold jewelry, or the clothing you wear—but let your adorning be the hidden person of the heart with the imperishable beauty of a gentle and quiet spirit, which in God's sight is very precious.

This is the sort of beauty they ought to look for. Yes, physical beauty is an important part of attraction, but physical beauty fades over time. The inner character that reflects the work of Christ in the one we love is of far greater importance. So tell your kids. Help them to understand why they should look to the inside and not the outside. Help them to believe the truth of Scripture, that what makes up a person's character is lasting. Remind them that they will be friends with their spouse for their entire life, sexy or not.

Creativity

Third, attraction to beauty is natural and not bad. But sexual attraction outside of a well-rounded relationship objectifies an image bearer and leads to sexual impurity. As we have been saying throughout the book, God created the world and made it beautiful. God created us with the ability to look at people and recognize his creative handiwork. Whether it is in the beauty of their character, their physical beauty, or both, God is a God who loves beauty (and at times makes odd things that are strangely beautiful). Noticing beauty is not a bad thing. But when we move from noticing beauty, thanking God for it, and then moving on with life, to dwelling on it in an unthankful manner, we objectify the person and remove their humanity. We take something that is beautiful and turn it into something that is ugly.

My (Joel's) former pastor used this helpful guide when talking to men about lust: "When we stop seeing a woman as an image bearer to be served, and start viewing her as an object to be used for our own sexual fulfillment, we are sinning." I have thought about that over the years, and it continues to ring true. When we look at pornography, what are we doing? Are we observing the beauty of an image bearer, thanking God for that beauty, and then moving on with life? Or are we using that man or woman as an object for fulfilling our own sexual pleasure? I think the answer is obvious. We don't just do this when we look at porn; we also do this when we look at people around us and linger. You can help your children (and yourself) by encouraging them to think properly about loving their neighbor instead of lusting after them.

Now it must be said that doing this 100 percent of the time is nearly impossible this side of glory. Saying to a teenage boy, "Don't lust" is like asking a pig to stay out of the mud. But as we will see in a moment, Jesus died to forgive our lustful desires, and if the Holy Spirit is at work in us and our teens, we have the power to fight against our sins. Lust and objectification are sins that like the dark—they like to hide. But when we bring them into the light through confession to God and others, we gain the forgiveness and support we need to fight our sins together, parent and child.

> Lust and objectification are sins that like the dark—they like to hide.

Dad, I'm not saying that if you look at porn, you should go confess to your teenage daughter. But your teens may have a greater propensity to come to you to confess and find help if you identify with them in their sins, telling them you understand what they are struggling with and then forgiving them. When you confess your sins to your kids, you are saying that you believe that even though your sin is great, God's grace is greater. You are proclaiming your trust in the Holy Spirit to help you as you struggle against this sin. Being open and honest about your own sin is one way to show your children how amazing God's goodness and grace are and how strong the Holy Spirit is.

Perspective

Fourth, remind your teens that there is a lot of life to live, and they don't know what it is to live a life together. Teens have about an inch of perspective and a mile of hormones. Their bodies are going through massive changes, and they think they're indestructible. They're the smartest human beings on the planet, and they need everything in life *right now*. They have no idea. This is such an old person thing to say, but we get to sit with them and help them understand that their perspective is necessarily extremely limited.

Now as with everything, there are ways to do this that are helpful and ways that push your teen away. When your teens are pouring out their lives to you, saying, "You have no idea what you're talking about" is not helpful. Trust me—I did it. It didn't work. But lovingly coming alongside your teens in a lifelong adventure, building bridges that allow you to shed some insight into their lives, goes a long way. Listening well to their concerns and giving carefully considered answers, or saying you don't know but will think about it, helps them to gain perspective on life. This is hard work because it takes a lot of time, it takes effort in studying and thinking about the issues your teen is facing, and it takes being dedicated to sticking with and loving your teen when their hormones are raging and they are unwilling to listen.

But this is exactly how Christ deals with us. When we complain because we don't get what we want, or we whine, "Why do I have to wait?" or "Why is this happening now?" the One with eternal perspective is lovingly dedicated to knowing us and walking with us over a lifetime in order to make us look more like Jesus. Paul Tripp often says, "God will take you where you haven't intended to go in order to produce in you what you wouldn't be able to produce on your own."[1]

Communicate Value

If we confess our sins, he is faithful and just to forgive us our sins.
1 JOHN 1:9

Last, have an open dialogue without belittling, getting angry, or being demeaning. This may be the most difficult thing to do. Our teens' concerns are real to them, and it is so easy to push those things to the side by being careless in our conversations with them. It is easy to get angry when our teen admits they like a person we may not particularly like. It is easy to demean them when they tell us of their attraction to another teen we have known for years. It is simple to belittle them when they struggle or tell you of their love for someone who is way out of their league.

These are easy things to do, but they are also mean. Instead of building bridges, they tear them down. If as you read this paragraph you are starting to get a sinking feeling in your stomach because this sounds like you, why don't you take a minute and confess your sins of pride and not loving your neighbor to Jesus right now? He will forgive them (1 John 1:9). Then go and confess your sins to your teen, and ask for their forgiveness for not loving them, hearing them, and valuing them. Then start the hard process of rebuilding the trust you have lost with them by listening, valuing their opinion, pushing back when necessary, and praying with and for them.

#friendgoals: Jesus, Friend of Sinners

I have called you friends.
JOHN 15:15

Here is the sad fact: All of our earthly friends will fail us. We will fail our teens, and they will fail us. As I write this, I (Joel) am experiencing this firsthand. Some of the people I thought I could count on are not the trustworthy friends I thought they were. Even my wonderful wife of 17 years, who is utterly amazing, cannot satisfy my need for friendship. And the scary thing is, I cannot do that for her either! That is the problem. Regardless of how big your friend group is or how good your sex life is, no earthly relationship will satisfy all your needs. It was never meant to. Our friends won't satisfy our desires, because they are sinners just like you and me. So what are we to do? We need to tell our kids that the desires they have for relational and sexual fulfillment are good, but ultimate satisfaction can be found only in Christ.

Jesus was and is so unexpected. He is a friend of sinners, tax collectors, drunks, prostitutes, pseudo law keepers, you, and me. All those passages about good friends we looked at earlier in this chapter describe Jesus's friendship with us. In Luke 24:13-35 Jesus explains to his disciples that the entire Old Testament is about him, so when we read that there is a friend who "sticks closer than a brother," that friend is Jesus. He is the friend we all desperately need, the one who will never fail us, the one who won't leave us. The friend who will always steer us in the right direction.

Jesus came to be friends with us—not with those who have it all together (do those people really exist?), but with those who are broken and need to have a friend who will stick with them through anything (Mark 2:15-17; Luke 7:31-34). Jesus came to be a friend to the outcast (Matthew 11:16-19). He came to seek out and save the lost (Luke 15:1-7; 19:10). He came to include losers and sinners in his friend group (Matthew 9:10-13). Jesus chose us in order to show us the love that a true friend has (John 15:12-17). This Jesus kills the #friendgoals. He is our #BFF, literally.

Encourage your teens to develop good, healthy friendships. Take notice when your kids practice building strong relationships. Model Christ's friendship to them. But most of all, point them to their ultimate friend, who alone can satisfy their souls.

Point them to their ultimate friend,
who alone can satisfy their souls.

Though Jesus hangs out with people who take advantage of others, he doesn't ever do that. Though his friend group consists of those people we would tell our kids to stay away from, he isn't influenced by them. Instead he changes them, just as he changes us. This is the friend we have in Jesus, the friend of sinners.

Words for Moms

This has been a tough situation in my own life. I know that it is superficial to judge people by their friends, but I have always judged my own life by the friends I keep, and I tend to do that with my kids too. It is not good enough for them or myself to have friends who are kind and are generally good company; they also have to be talented and good looking. I want for my kids what I want for myself—a friend group that somehow confirms worth and value. I have been chasing this for fortyish years, and I see the futility in it, but I continue the chase myself and have to fight against putting pressure on my children to join in. We need the Holy Spirit to do a work in our hearts first, and then we are better equipped to help our kids.

Our message to our children needs to be that Jesus Christ is their friend. That what they are looking for from friends, even from boyfriends or girlfriends, is found in him. They are loved and understood without having to prove themselves or measure up. It is important to help your kids see that friendships with the opposite sex don't have to lead to romance. Let them see the value in having different types of friends. Affirm that friendship is incredibly important. We don't have to be afraid.

If this is an area you need to talk to your kids about, if you have been too controlling or you haven't given enough input, now is the time to do something about it. Get to know their friends. Ask what they like best about them. But always make sure they understand that what their friends think of them isn't the most important thing. Jesus calls them friends in John 15:15. Point out the beauty of that truth and ask the Holy Spirit to make that truth beautiful in your own eyes as well.

Words for Dads

It is a lonely time to be a man in our culture. Friendship among men isn't a topic that gets much attention. We start out as kids with friends, we go through middle school and high school with friends, we even graduate from college with friends, and then we enter the workforce, get married...and stop having friends. We need to reevaluate the role of friends in our lives. You may be fine with no friends, or you may be lonely. Friendship and relationship is key for all of us. Whether you or your kids have realized it, learning how to build good friendships now is important if they are to develop healthy relationships in the future.

We want them to plug in with the sort of people who will encourage them in their walk with Christ. We need to help them understand that the most important characteristic of a friend is not their appearance or athletic ability or sense of humor. We need to encourage them to be friends who are fun, but more importantly, who value Christ.

Dad, it is time to tell your teens that Jesus is their truest friend. He is the friend who will never leave them, never gossip about them, never make fun of them. This friendship is so much more valuable than anything any earthly friendship can offer.

TALKING POINTS

This is going to be an ongoing conversation in your household. You and your teens may not have considered the way our friendships inform our view of sex. Here are some talking points to help get the conversation going.

- Jesus didn't come just to befriend the good people. He was known as a friend of sinners. It may be helpful to ask your children who Jesus's friends would be if he were on earth today.

- Friendship is of great value in a sexual relationship. It is often more important and deeper than the actual act of sex.

- Ask your teens what they like about certain friends. Seeing the good in others is helpful for all of us.

- Friends will come and go. Jesus is the only completely true and faithful friend.

6

Likes and Comments
How Social Media Is Shaping Our Teens

*The fear of man lays a snare, but
whoever trusts in the Lord is safe.*
PROVERBS 29:25

Ira Glass, the host of a podcast called *This American Life*, once interviewed three teenage girls as they posted selfies on Instagram.[1] He asked them what they thought would happen once they posted the pictures.

They replied that usually there are at least two likes in a minute, but they pointed out that it's not the best time of day for posting pics because people might not be on social media. Ira noted, "What they are waiting for is not just likes and comments. They want a specific kind of comment." They want "comments from other girls, and the wording is pretty much always the same."

The girls listed some of the words they are looking for from the other girls. "Gorgeous. Pretty. Stunning. You kill it. You're so pretty. So beautiful."

Ira asked for clarification about these comments. Are they posted regardless of what the picture looks like? The girls affirm that this is the case, and they went on to tell him that the language is so complimentary, it's almost like a contest to see who can say the nicest thing about the picture. The girls mentioned that their moms don't understand why everyone posts the same comments or why the girls need to constantly hear that they are pretty.

Ira then explained that the Instagram comments are about social standing within a group. These girls—and your girls and my (Jessica's) daughter—are all looking for a constant reassurance of their place in their group of friends. The most important thing about the comments is who is doing the commenting. The girls explained that the comments let everyone know who your friends are, and the closeness of the friendship is displayed by how complimentary the comments are. You can reciprocate the feelings of friendship by commenting back to the person. How you comment back and what your comment says means a lot to these girls. Even the timing of the response is important.

In the podcast, the girls eventually admitted, "There is definitely a weird psychology to it."

Ira then asked if the girls have "gotten into weird mind games" with their friends on social media. The three girls answered unanimously with a strong yes. They went on to discuss how mindless the comments are because they are all posting them on everyone's pictures all the time.

Ira asked if this process makes them feel good even though they know it is a rote activity. Again all the girls answered yes. But then they also admitted that when a girl posts an unflattering selfie, they take screen shots of it and send it to each other so that they can laugh at the girl. They talked about how they each send selfies that they are about to post to other friends and ask if they should post them so they won't be made fun of.

Ira lamented that they seem to have full-time jobs with social media, and one of the girls responded, "It's like I'm a brand and I am trying to promote myself," and "To stay relevant you have to work."

This is what our kids are dealing with every single day. They are looking to stay relevant in their social circles. This is where we parents need to be mindful and help our kids see that their worth is not tied to comments or likes.

"Please don't post that on Insta!"

"Why not?"

"I look terrible!"

"So what? You are beautiful!"

"NOOO!"

I cannot tell you how many times I have heard this conversation around me. The question I have always asked myself and my kids is, why would it matter? What is it about social media platforms that makes us desire to put our best self in front of others? To angle the cell phone just right, 120 degrees above our heads, the sun shining on our face, only cool stuff in the background, and no one better looking than us in the photo. Or maybe you have just gotten to the gym, and you want to take a #sexy #instafit photo. So you stand in front of the mirror, snap the selfie, and post it sharing a view that you may not be willing to share in any other context. I mean, really, at what point in the history of man have we ever thought it was sexy to see a picture of someone in the bathroom? This unprecedented view into other people's worlds gives everyone access to see and judge parts of our lives that people have never had access to.

What are we trying to do with all this? What are our teens looking for when they go on social media and post intimate information about themselves? Is it okay? Am I just old? Why do I keep asking questions?

We have affirmed that the love and attention that our kids are after can be found only in Christ. But the false affirmation that our kids get from social media points to a desire that is inside all of us. This desire to be affirmed, to be loved, is something we all identify with, and right now those feelings are being met superficially online.

This desire to be affirmed, to be loved, is something we all identify with, and right now those feelings are being met superficially online.

This new community is actually quite old, and it is not all bad. For better or worse, we need to think carefully about social media platforms like Instagram, Twitter, Facebook, and Snapchat. In this chapter we want to help you think about some of the impact we see in our own spheres of influence as a pastor and a speaker.

Unprecedented Access

We live in a time when we are comfortable with people knowing many details of our lives. When we go to get our hair cut, we post a picture. When we buy new clothes, we post a picture. When we try them on, we post a picture. Brushing hair? Post a picture. These harmless pictures don't really matter, but they give people access to more and more of our lives. There is instant access to parts of our kids' lives that people never had the ability to see before.

This is not a bad thing. I just found out that a close friend of mine secretly went to Vegas and got married. It was awesome. Without social media, I would never have known that. We find out prayer requests, we see pictures of graduations. All of this unprecedented access to the events in each other's lives draws us closer and keeps us connected.

Social media also provides a way for oppressed people who have no other way to voice their fears and concerns to be heard. Think about the Arab Spring without Twitter or the Black Lives Matter movement without Facebook live. These platforms have provided a place for us to coalesce around a cause, to be exposed to injustice, to learn how to get involved. This access also gives us insight into how we can offer support to our friends when they are struggling, how we can grieve with those in our friend group who have experienced loss, and how to pray for those who suffer.

But there is also an increasing expectation placed on our kids to let people into parts of their lives that no one would have had access to before. Whether it is the changing room or the bathroom or, even worse, the bedroom. There is no mystery to kids' lives, no expectation of privacy, no place where they are not being watched, photographed, and shared. This breeds a performance mentality and a filtered or curated picture of their lives. In the past, looking into these private parts of people's lives would have been called voyeurism. Now it's just normal life.

In the past, looking into these private parts of people's lives would have been called voyeurism. Now it's just normal life.

Social media is also allowing people to voice their opinions about everything from the way their hair is styled and the look of their nails, to politics and moral issues. In doing this they are giving people unprecedented access to parts of their hearts that their second cousin's friend would never have been able to access. Even with private accounts, our kids are opening themselves up to acquaintances and listening to those people's opinions as if they were their best friends.

This unprecedented access exposes not only our private lives but also our desires, our hearts. These are not just isolated pictures but a collage of ourselves that shows us as fun, funny, sexy, smart, fitness minded, socially conscious, popular, and well loved. The pictures expose our desire to be a certain person, an idealized you. No one wants to face the fact that they have pimples, or worse yet, fat dimples. Notice that you typically don't see pictures of people picking their noses, but you know they do!

What is all this about? Danah Boyd, in her book *It's Complicated: The Social Media Lives of Networked Teens*, points out that for our teens, it's about finding a community that affirms them, finding friends. I came away from her book thinking that they are not searching for anything new—they want to feel worthy of love and praise.

Here is the interesting thing: The aspects of social media that scare us so much are not new. When I (Joel) was a kid, I wanted to find worth with my friends, so I conformed to the image that brought me acceptance. When I was a teen, I tried to become my own person, and in doing so I struck out from the safety of my parents. I dyed my hair purple, wore jeans that had huge holes in them, listened to really loud punk rock music, and was a hooligan. What my kids do today is not very different from what I did—they are finding a community where they fit in even with all their unique characteristics. They are trying to find worth.

Finding Worth

Take delight in honoring each other.
Romans 12:10 nlt

Much has been written correlating the rise of depression, anxiety, sleeplessness, and even suicide with the overuse of social media.[2] Some kids are predisposed to experience some of these issues, but there is no doubt that these problems are more likely to occur when our kids are basing their opinion of themselves, their beauty, and their self-worth on the opinions of others.

This presses them. It makes them live for the affirmation of their friend groups. Constantly living for the approval of others forces them into a thin existence, an existence that doesn't allow them to explore who they are and to find their value in the love of their family, the church, and Christ.

In the world of social media, our kids are worthy of love and kindness, not because they are image bearers but because of how they look or what they wear. This is when it matters that we are involved in our children's lives. Our words matter. Our love matters. Our affirmations of their worth help them to be settled in who they are. We need to tell them they are worthy not only because they look beautiful but also because they are kind, creative, funny, smart, interesting, and so on. But most of all we need to affirm the progress we see in them as they grow into adulthood and into the image of Christ. It is all too easy to focus on what they are doing wrong and to use that snapshot to draw conclusions about their future. But when we do that, we are providing the same sort of feedback they are getting online.

I (Jessica) like to call this being a grace detective. Actively look for things you can affirm in your child's life—things you can encourage them in. It is really easy for us to see all the things they are doing wrong, especially if those things affect us. I mean, how hard is it to put a dish in the dishwasher? But how often are you actively looking for ways to encourage them?

"Hey, I noticed you started to get angry at your sister earlier but held back and didn't say anything unkind. Thanks for that."

"Thank you for putting your dish in the dishwasher."

"Babe, I see you have been turning all of your homework in. Great job."

My encouragement to you is to search out things you can validate in your child's life. It might be really hard if your kid is in a tough spot, but ask the Lord to help you see them with fresh eyes. Pray that he will help you acknowledge when they, by the grace of God, do something commendable. Paul tells us in Romans 12:10 to "take delight in honoring each other" (NLT). Kind words go a long way when kids feel as if they aren't being seen. Most of us feel that way, so why would we think our kids are any different?

> My encouragement to you is to search out things you can validate in your child's life.

You're Gorgeous

The other day I (Joel) was going through my daughter's Instagram feed (she knows I do this) and looking at the comments people were leaving on each other's pictures. There was so much pat affirmation; I had to wonder how much of it was real. How much of it was written just because it was expected to be written? It was a reciprocal relationship. One friend would write, "You're so beautiful," to which the person would reply, "You're beyond gorgeous." Then someone replies with the heart-eyes emoji. This sort of discourse happens on most posts regardless of whether the person is gorgeous.

This sort of back-and-forth plays an important part in the dynamics of social media. In the digital world, this is how people know who is a friend and where they fit in the overall scheme of things. But the problem is that the only image we see and comment on is a curated image of themselves. And while these comments are meant to affirm, they teach a subtle lesson: A person's worth is based on how many likes or kind comments they receive online. They begin to depend on them, going back and checking their posts repeatedly to see what people have said or if people have liked their photos.

Also, on a darker side, social media outlets allow a forum for teens to show parts of their bodies they would normally never show in public. Not all teens are looking to be sexually active on social media. But there is no denying the fact that social media is providing a forum for the propagation of pornography. We consider this topic in the next chapter, but for now, note that sex sells on social media.

When our teens post pictures that show them in various states of dress with the hashtag #sexy, they are looking for affirmation, but they don't realize they are participating in a system that will commodify them, reducing them to objects for lust. Whether it is a teen boy posting a picture of his six pack with his pants practically falling off, or a teenage girl posting a belfie—a butt selfie—the sort of affirmation they are looking for will actually leave them feeling dirty and wanting something more.

> When our teens post pictures that show them in various states of dress with the hashtag #sexy, they are looking for affirmation, but they don't realize they are participating in a system that will commodify them, reducing them to objects for lust.

Kids want to be seen with the right people. The right boy or girl can catapult them into a different social stratum. To have their picture liked or commented on by the right person places them in a different sphere. To have their picture ignored by their friends is seen as a failure and is often taken as a statement.

But let's be honest. It is not just our kids who are subject to the tyranny of the like. We live under the oppression of the same taskmaster. We post something—maybe a quote out of a book or a picture of a craft. Or worse, we tell others what we are doing and conversations we have had in order to find affirmation. I (Joel) cannot tell you how often I have fished for a compliment after teaching or preaching. I try to present a public image of a smart and yet sufficiently humble pastor.

People say things like, "Oh, Pastor, that was so good. Again. I just love it when you preach."

And I say things like, "Oh, Parishioner, I am just a humble servant of the great King Jesus." #humblebrag

It is ridiculous! I'm living for the approval of others just as much as my kids are. Instead of hoping people will say, "You're gorgeous" (which would be odd), I look for people to build me up in other ways and give me the affirmation I want in order to feel valuable.

We all desire to be affirmed. That is why we dress the way we dress, speak the way we do, and hang out with the people we hang with. We all desire to be affirmed.

The Settled Self

Your Maker is your husband.

ISAIAH 54:5

The idea of the settled self has been floating around for a while now. It is easier to conjure an image of a settled person than it is to describe one. The settled person is the person who walks into a room and doesn't need to be seen with the most important people. They don't put on a front in order to be liked. They are their own person. This person doesn't act for other people's approval. They are settled with who they are, and they love others out of that settledness. They are not aloof, but engage with each person individually. They are not rushed, they enjoy being with you, and they are not looking for a more important conversation.

This is the sort of person who stands up to injustice, not to be seen on social media but because they believe standing up to injustice is the right thing to do. They don't feel as if they have to make a big deal out of being a Christian, but they don't hide it either.

They are secure. They are not looking for the affirmation of others to make them feel worthy of love and praise. They actively praise God and love the saints. They are settled in who they are in Christ and how Jesus loves them.

I'm thinking of a woman who grew up in my church. As she has grown older, she has become more and more beautiful. She does not show any need to find her security or worth in anything or anyone but Christ. That is not to say she is perfect or has reached complete communion with Christ. But she is settled in who she is. Does she have insecurities? I'm sure she does. But she is settled.

What makes a person settled in who they are? Is it getting a like or a comment saying they are beautiful? No, that won't ever be able to do it. How do we know? Because teens keep posting photos and looking for comments to affirm them.

So what will provide what our teens need in order to feel settled about themselves? Only this—to recognize that Jesus provides us with everything we need, and we can receive it by faith. Jesus gives us the very things we desire, everything we require to be settled—his love, his affirmation, his very kingdom—because Jesus gives us himself. He unites us to himself, and in doing so he gives us more than just a like or a comment. He gives us himself in marriage. All the things we desire most are found in Jesus.

> Jesus gives us the very things we desire, everything we require to be settled—his love, his affirmation, his very kingdom—because Jesus gives us himself.

Jared C. Wilson, in his book *The Imperfect Disciple: Grace for Those Who Cannot Get Their Act Together*, talks about this desire to be fulfilled. In the last chapter he quotes from a George Whitefield sermon titled "Christ, the Best Husband."

> Consider who the Lord Jesus is, whom you are invited to espouse yourselves unto; he is the best husband; there is none comparable to Jesus Christ.
>
> Do you desire one that is great? He is of the highest dignity, he is the glory of heaven, the darling of eternity, admired by angels, dreaded by devils, and adored by saints. For you

to be espoused to so great a king, what honor will you have by this espousal?

Do you desire one that is rich? None is comparable to Christ, the fullness of the earth belongs to him. If you be espoused to Christ, you shall share in his unsearchable riches; you shall receive of his fullness, even grace for grace here, and you shall hereafter be admitted to glory, and shall live with this Jesus to all eternity.

Do you desire one that is wise? There is none comparable to Christ for wisdom. His knowledge is infinite, and his wisdom is correspondent thereto. And if you are espoused to Christ, he will guide and counsel you, and make you wise unto salvation.

Do you desire one that is potent, who may defend you against your enemies, and all the insults and reproaches of the Pharisees of this generation? There is none that can equal Christ in power; for the Lord Jesus Christ hath all power.

Do you desire one that is good? There is none like unto Christ in this regard; others may have some goodness, but it is imperfect; Christ's goodness is complete and perfect, he is full of goodness and in him dwelleth no evil.

Do you desire one that is beautiful? His eyes are most sparkling, his looks and glances of love are ravishing, his smiles are most delightful and refreshing unto the soul: Christ is the most lovely person of all others in the world.

Do you desire one that can love you? None can love you like Christ: His love, my dear sisters, is incomprehensible; his love passeth all other loves: The love of the Lord Jesus is first, without beginning; his love is free without any motive; his love is great without any measure; his love is constant without any change, and his love is everlasting.[3]

What Whitefield is saying and what we are saying is that Jesus is the only one in the universe who can meet all our needs and bring lasting satisfaction. A relationship with Jesus is the only thing in the universe that settles us and transforms us from consumers of each other, from people who live off each other's affirmation, to people who are settled in him.

> A relationship with Jesus is the only thing in the universe that settles us and transforms us from consumers of each other, from people who live off each other's affirmation, to people who are settled in him.

Finding Our All in Christ

Christ is all, and in all.

Colossians 3:11

As you help settle your kids in who they are in Christ, it may seem too simple to actually do what you hope it will do, but the gospel is simple. It is not the gospel that is complicated; it is believing it and resting in it that are so very difficult, especially for teens who are facing their raging hormones, their fickle friends, their desires to be liked, their longing to be loved, and their changing place in the world. But this should be nothing new to us. Even as we write this book, we find it difficult to believe that everything we need relationally, everything we want from others, we already have in Christ. So let's take a moment to rehearse the gospel so we are on the same page and so you can use this as a cheat sheet for talking to your teen.

First, we are all dead in our sin—not only the sins we commit personally but also the sin we inherited from Adam (Romans 5:12-14; Ephesians 2:1-3). This is true for your teen as well as you, and it's key when talking to your kids. Whether your sin de jour was (or is) sexual sin, anger, pride, greed, or lust, you and your teen are in the same place. You both approach the cross as sinners in need of God's mercy. Before you became a Christian, your purity and good works could not earn you anything before God. You were born under the law and were required to keep it perfectly, but of course, no one ever has except Jesus. The apostle Paul says in Galatians 3:23, "Now before faith came, we were held captive under the law, imprisoned until the coming faith would be revealed."

If you approach your kids as if you have no sin, you deny 1 John 1:8, which tells us, "If we say we have no sin, we deceive ourselves, and the truth is not in us." This is true not only before we are Christians but afterward as well. We all come to Christ on level ground. This humbles us, and when our teens see that humility, they are more likely to be receptive to our instruction. You know this to be true. Imagine that I caught you sinning and said to you, "Get your act together. Can't you stop being angry? Why do you do this? How could you?" You wouldn't be likely to listen, because I wouldn't be talking with you, I would be talking at you. There is no humility in this, just anger and arrogance. This brings us to the second part of the gospel.

Yes, we are all sinners, but God the Father took it upon himself to send Jesus the Son to live under the law. Galatians 4:4-5 says, "When the fullness of time had come, God sent forth his Son, born of woman, born under the law, to redeem those who were under the law, so that we might receive adoption as sons." Jesus came and was born a man.

> The Word became flesh and dwelt among us, and we have seen his glory, glory as of the only Son from the Father, full of grace and truth. (John bore witness about him, and cried out, "This was he of whom I said, 'He who comes after me ranks before me, because he was before me.'") For from his fullness we have all received, grace upon grace. For the law was given through Moses; grace and truth came through Jesus Christ. No one has ever seen God; the only God, who is at the Father's side, he has made him known (John 1:14-18).

Jesus was a man, born under the law so he could keep the law as a man for all of us. He did what we never could do, living a sinless life and keeping the law on our behalf (Romans 5:18-21). Jesus's active obedience is credited to us so that we are counted righteous before God. This leads us to a deep humility before God and others. Even your righteousness as a believer does not make you righteous before God. Only Jesus's righteousness given to you does that. When you talk to your kids, help them to be grounded in the active obedience of Christ. Don't excuse their sin, but tell them their right standing with God comes only through faith in Jesus.

But God didn't just stop there. Jesus's active obedience gives us righteousness before God, but the penalty of sin still needs to be paid. Our sin deserves God's wrath. In the Garden, God told Adam and Eve that they would surely die when they sinned. Our sin deserves physical death and eternal death in hell. In Matthew 18:9 Jesus says, "If your eye causes you to sin, tear it out and throw it away. It is better for you to enter life with one eye than with two eyes to be thrown into the hell of fire."[4] But Jesus died in order to free us from the penalty of sin. "For our sake he made him to be sin who knew no sin, so that in him we might become the righteousness of God" (2 Corinthians 5:21). Romans 8 tells us that through Christ's death we are now free from the condemnation that comes with our failure to keep God's law.

This good news can give your kids hope. Every time they go to social media to find their worth, every time they read the comments to be affirmed, you can remind them that through Jesus they have already received the most important comments they will ever read or hear. They are God's children. Adopted. Loved. Cared for. Gorgeous in his sight!

> Every time they go to social media to find their worth, every time they read the comments to be affirmed, you can remind them that through Jesus they have already received the most important comments they will ever read or hear.

But the good news doesn't stop there. This would all be great enough as it is, but Jesus was raised from the dead to confirm the fact that all this is true (1 Corinthians 15). Romans 4:25 says that Jesus was "raised for our justification." Jesus was raised so that our standing with God would be "just as if" we had never sinned. This brings hope to your kids and to you. Dear sinner saved by grace, this is what is true of you. Because Jesus lived the life we could never live, because he died the death we deserved and was raised on the third day, we stand in his righteousness before God. "Who is to condemn? Christ Jesus is the one who died—more than that, who was raised—who is at the right hand of God, who indeed is interceding for us" (Romans 8:34).

Last but certainly not least, Jesus right now is praying for you and your teen. Jesus is praying that you and your teen would be conformed into his image through these talks. He is praying for you to have strength and boldness. He is praying for your teens to put off sin and put on righteousness. He is praying that they would know the power of his resurrection. He is praying for you! And Jesus's prayers never fall on deaf ears. Praise God that he cares that much for you and for your teen.

> Jesus right now is praying for you and your teen...
> and Jesus's prayers never fall on deaf ears.

Don't hold this back from your kids. I know the fear that is in your heart, because it's in my heart too. If I tell this to them, they will go and have sex. But that is the opposite of what the gospel does inside us. The apostle Paul anticipated this argument in Romans 6:1-14. He tells us that when we have faith in Christ, we are not to continue to sin because sin no longer has dominion over us. Sin is no longer the dominating factor in our lives. Sin has lost its power over us.

Yes, your teen may struggle with sexual sin, but there is forgiveness available that breaks sin's power. First John 1:9 tells us how this happens: "If we confess our sins, he is faithful and just to forgive us our sins and to cleanse us from all unrighteousness." The sin that would try to condemn our teens, the sin that would try to condemn us, is forgiven when we repent of it. No qualifications, no penance. Jesus promises that if we are believers in Christ, he will, through the power of his Spirit, complete the work in us (see Philippians 1:6).

This good news, this gospel, has upheld us. It will uphold you and will keep your teens. Give them this freedom, give them this hope. Give them this gospel, especially when they fall. Ground them in this gospel so they don't have to chase their identity through social media.

Words for Moms

You can surely relate to the desire to be loved and affirmed. My guess is that you, too, engage in social media. We post pictures of our kids, our houses, our pets, our meals, our quiet times...all with the hope that we will gain the approval of certain people.

Now, don't get me wrong, I am not against social media at all—I actually really love it. I love seeing what people are up to. I love letting people know what's going on in my life. My main motivating factor when posting is not to gain approval, but I would be lying if I said if that desire wasn't in there somewhere.

So as we ourselves struggle to find the settled self, we can be honest about that with our kids. Let your teens know you understand the temptation to get approval and identity from what others think of you. Share specific stories with them of how you do this. Don't just feed them the "I get it" line. Open up your life to them within reason. Don't be afraid to let them know you are in this with them.

We have been careful in this book not to make a list of what you should and should not do with your kids, or to tell you what you should or should not let your kids do. Instead, we want you to learn with your kids. Pay attention to how they learn, their likes and dislikes. Parenting isn't a one-size-fits-all endeavor. Pour out your love on them even though you will never be able to give your children all the love and affection they need. You are not capable of it. Which is why it is so important to ground them in the love of Christ for sinners.

Talk with your kids about identity issues. Talk with them about porn. Talk with them about body issues. Don't let any topic be off-limits. These conversations will be uncomfortable at first, but the more you engage, the more natural they will be.

Words for Dads

Dad, you may think that social media is not that important, that what people say about our teens online is inconsequential. This could not be further from the truth. Our teens are looking for affirmation, for acceptance from their peers.

Before you dismiss that, think about how you desire the same things. On the job, you work hard and stay late to be affirmed with a raise or a promotion. Or you buck the system in order to gain acceptance from the rebels. We all struggle with these desires. Be open with your teen about your struggles. Talk with them about how they are accepted in Christ and secure in your love.

If you have a teenage daughter, don't just affirm her when she looks beautiful. Build your daughter up in her relationship with Christ. Tell her that Jesus loves her regardless of whether she fits society's mold. Then build her up in her ability, praise her for her intellect, compliment her athletic prowess. Build her up in Christ and help her to understand that she is beautiful, loved, and secure even if she doesn't get any likes on social media.

If you have teen boys, warn them of the dangers of judging people by what they look like. Warn them of the dangers of trying to be liked through a social media account. Ground them in the truth that their manhood isn't measured by the number of followers they have or the beauty of the girls who like their photos. Their identity is in Christ. He values them. He sticks with them. He loves them.

TALKING POINTS

Don't let social media scare you into doing too much about it or doing too little about it. Engage your kids on the topic of social media. Ask lots of questions. We aren't young and hip anymore, so we need to ask our kids about it and to do our own research on anything we don't understand.

- Social media is not necessarily good or bad. The way we use it and what we use it for can be good or bad.

- We must find our identity in what God says about us instead of how many likes and comments we get on a post.

- Affirm your kids for more than their physical appearance.

- Ask your children why they enjoy social media or what they get out of it.

- Every emotional need we desire is fulfilled in what Christ has done for us.

- Justification—"just as if I had never sinned" and "just as if I had always obeyed"—will help your child find his or her settled self.

7

Over-Sexualization
How Pornography and the Distancing of Relationships Are Hurting Our Teens

Do you not know that the unrighteous will not inherit the kingdom of God? Do not be deceived: neither the sexually immoral, nor idolaters, nor adulterers, nor men who practice homosexuality, nor thieves, nor the greedy, nor drunkards, nor revilers, nor swindlers will inherit the kingdom of God. And such were some of you. But you were washed, you were sanctified, you were justified in the name of the Lord Jesus Christ and by the Spirit of our God.

1 CORINTHIANS 6:9–11

Sex is everywhere. It is hard to escape. Music, movies, TV...even cartoons aren't safe. In kids' movies, it is hinted at if not overtly suggested. The cartoon network show *Steven Universe* pushes this sexualization to new areas as children's shows call into question gender roles and sexuality.[1] But the creators of this show are not charting a new course. They are following in a long line of shows that have pushed sex on our kids either overtly or covertly.

I (Joel) cannot remember this happening in my cartoons, but now as an adult I have been showing my kids the programs I used to watch, and it is everywhere. The older brother in *The Last Starfighter* has a stash of *Playboy*s. The hockey team in *The Mighty Ducks* steals a box of *Sports Illustrated Swimsuit* issues and passes them around. It was everywhere when I was a kid.

Now there are realistic sex dolls that are programmed to respond to touch and submit to rape and all sorts of deviancy. This is the world we are living in. Gender is being challenged and is seen as fluid. In the Netflix show *The OA*, one of the characters is transitioning as a young teen. The teen literature book *Luna*, a National Book Award finalist, tells the fictional tale of a young boy who is transitioning to be a girl. This is not to say our culture is going to hell in a handbasket but rather that the topic of sex is everywhere in our culture and is aimed directly at our teens.

Recently, I (Joel) showed the movie *Wonder Woman* to the youth at the church where I am a pastor. I am always trying to help teens at church learn how to engage culture, and *Wonder Woman* is a fun movie and a huge cultural touch point for our teens. In this movie, Diana (played by Gal Gadot) walks in on Steve Trevor (played by Chris Pine) coming out of the bath. The dialogue includes an awkward tension and a not-so-covert reference to the size of his penis. They continue to discuss the nature of relationships when the two of them are in a boat sailing toward the war, and Diana and Trevor talk about sex.

> Diana: You don't sleep with women?
>
> Steve: I do sleep with women, I do sleep...Yes, I do. But out of the confines of marriage it's just...it's...not polite to assume, you know.
>
> Diana: Marriage?
>
> Steve: You don't have that, do you? You go before a judge and you swear to love, honor and uh, cherish each other until death do you part.
>
> Diana: And do they? Love each other till death?
>
> Steve: Not very often, no.

Diana: Then why do they do it?

Steve: I have no idea.

Diana: So you cannot sleep with me unless I marry you?

Steve: I'll sleep with you if you want. I'll sleep right there.

Diana: There is plenty of room.

Steve: Then fine…

A few moments later, the dialogue continues.

Diana: The pleasures of the flesh…

Steve: You know about that?

Diana: I have read all 12 volumes of Cleo's treatises on worldly pleasure.

Steve: All 12? Huh, did you bring any of those with you?

Diana: You would not enjoy them.

Steve: I don't know about that.

Diana: No, you wouldn't.

Steve: Why not?

Diana: They came to the conclusion that men were essential for procreation, but when it comes to pleasure… unnecessary.

Steve: No, no.

Diana: Goodnight.[2]

Exposure

It is amazing what our teens are being exposed to. The rapid sexualization of our culture has seemingly come out of nowhere. In the past, if you were going to find pornography, you had to go looking for it in magazines or on scrambled channels. Now our teens are able to find pornography with the click of a button and are even creating it.

In her book *American Girls: Social Media and the Secret Lives of Teenagers*, Nancy Jo Sales traces the way teenage American girls interact with social media. She points out the stark reality of a porn aesthetic, beauty that is run through eyes that are shaped by pornography. We see this when 13-year-old girls get padded bras and wear revealing clothes. A 13-year-old girl should never be looked at and evaluated on how big her breasts look! That is just sick.

I don't want my 13-year-old daughter to be swallowed by a system that looks at her only as a sexual being. I don't want her to be looked at by teen boys or older men as an object to be undressed in their minds. This is a source of serious self-loathing for some girls, and that must be taken into account when we seek to ground them in the beauty that Christ has given them. We have to be careful to do what we can to keep them from falling into the porn aesthetic.

Because of websites dedicated to porn and the prevalence of social media, our kids are seeing images at younger and younger ages that will shape them for the rest of their lives. This exposure changes the way their brain works and the way they think about sex and the opposite sex.

Objectification

Let us make man in our image, after our likeness.
GENESIS 1:26

The ugly reality is that the influx of pornography feeds the tendency to lust. As a result, when boys look at girls on social media, they see them as objects to be used to fulfill their desires, not as bearers of God's image. One interview of 13-year-old girls prompted these responses:

> "A lot of boys are like, if you don't have boobs and a butt, they don't like you," Maggie said.

> "That's most of the boys right now," said Cassy.

> "A lot of the boys in this generation—boys are not looking at the personality," said Julie.

"They're just looking at the boobs and butt," Cassy said. "And if you don't have them they won't date you."[3]

The proliferation of porn, the expression of our personhood through pictures, the overemphasis on sex...these influences devalue our relationships and turn people into objects for use. When was the last time you heard a pop song lauding the beauty of a person's personality regardless of their physical appearance?

Porn places emphasis on the size and use of certain body parts—for both women and men. If that is where our teen boys learn about the role of sex in relationships, they will naturally see women as objects to use sexually. This dangerous misperception is reinforced if teen boys see their dads viewing porn rather than developing true intimacy with their wives. Boys can be led to thinking that any walk in the park can turn into a sexual encounter. It is insanity!

I (Joel) could relate horror story after horror story of men who have been trapped in a lifetime of porn use and the resulting destruction of relationships. But this warning too often falls on deaf ears. Teens need to be shown how to respect the opposite sex and to appreciate true beauty, which isn't based on a person's looks.

> Teens need to be shown how to respect the opposite sex and to appreciate true beauty, which isn't based on a person's looks.

The church is not immune from this problem. Famous pastors have encouraged women to get breast implants to please their men and to do anything their husbands want them to do sexually. Men are pressured to look a certain way, to be fitness freaks, and to fulfill their wives' fantasies. This is an unbiblical and abusive capitulation to the porn aesthetic by shepherds who should be leading the sheep into lives of love for God and neighbor (Ezekiel 34).

Our churches ought to be places where our kids are not subject to this aesthetic, but are protected from it. They should be places where people who have been caught in the snare of porn can be restored, forgiven, and healed. Everyone in this world has lusted, but Jesus forgives those who lust.

Make no bones about it: Pornography is sin. We need to tell our kids that viewing pornography is sinful because of the lust it creates and the slavery it promotes. Let's provide our kids with something better.

Dehumanization

When we are driven by our lusts and our out-of-control desires tempt us to look at porn, we forget that the people in the pictures are human beings. They are real people with real hopes and dreams. They are someone's daughters, someone's sons. They were raised in homes and grew up wanting to be loved, to be affirmed in who they are.

When we watch people have sex, we don't think in these terms. We just want to use them to give us a thrill. They become things, not humans. This is increasingly true as the sexual acts become more deviant. We would never refer to our daughters or sons in the terms people use for porn actors.

Throughout history, people have denied other people's human dignity, value, and worth to justify taking advantage of those other people for their own ends. How could people excuse keeping slaves and treating them harshly? How could civilizations rationalize treating women and children merely as pieces of property? How can our own country abort babies for the sake of convenience and "the right to choose"? People do these things when they see others not as human beings but as objects for use.

We need to help our teens see that the people who are acting in these porn films did not set out to live this life. Let's demonstrate to our teens how we can humanize each other again. Let's help our teens see porn actors as human beings in need of God's mercy, grace, and love. Let's help our teens pray for them. When we humanize the actors, we are less likely to use them. They will no longer be two-dimensional images on a screen to be used for our teens' pleasure, but real people who are searching for satisfaction but blinded by their sin.

Trafficking

Those who produce and use pornography are perpetuating a system of sin. A system that hides in the dark. Porn preys on people, taking advantage of them and entrapping them. The dark secret behind porn is the system of sex trafficking that provides the steady supply of men, women, and children to fulfill users' fantasies. Yes, some people are willing participants, signing up to participate in porn and prostitution. But there is growing evidence that the increased use of pornography, sex trafficking, and prostitution are all linked.[4] Women and children are being trafficked for use in porn.[5]

To make matters even worse, the longer people are exposed to porn, the more deviant their porn use gets. These deviant practices then become so normalized that men expect their wives to perform the same acts they are watching. These include demeaning acts that degrade their spouses instead of building them up. This is clearly seen in the bestselling book and movie *50 Shades of Grey*. This book glorifies men's dominance of women and normalizes demeaning acts, and it is shaping this pornographic aesthetic.

Of course, not everyone who looks at pornography is trafficking humans. But they are contributing to the horrific system, so the link between the two sins must be brought to light. We live in a time when social justice and social concerns are on our teens' minds. Kids galvanize behind causes. Yet the church rarely talks about this massive injustice.

When we talk to our teens, we need to help them see that when they view porn, they are participating in a system that oppresses people, and that is a sin against a perfectly holy God. When they view porn online, even if it is free, their clicks pay for the cost of people to be enslaved.

Let's show kids a better way. First, we can encourage them to come to Christ and find forgiveness in him by confessing their sins. King David talks of this in Psalm 32, in which (many scholars believe) David repents for viewing Bathsheba nude, sleeping with her, and murdering her husband. Next, we can encourage kids to turn away from the sins of lust and looking at pornography and instead to fight for those who are trafficked. Finally, we can encourage them to help their friends who are addicted to porn by showing their friends the way to forgiveness and freedom in Christ.

Distance

The use of pornography also creates distance in relationships. When our teens become accustomed to interacting with a 2D image, they lose the ability to relate to a flesh-and-blood person. Many have reported fear and depression when considering relationships because they do not know how to relate to someone of the opposite sex.

This is leading to distance between teen boys who regularly use porn and girls who would have in the past been the objects of their affection. The *Telegraph* published an article titled "Why teenagers' obsession with porn is creating a generation of 20-year-old virgins."[6] Normally I would be happy about a generation of kids who are not sexually active, but these kids are abstaining not because they don't want to sin but because they are seeking the pleasure of sex without the work of building a relationship. Porn normalizes loneliness. It makes isolation easy. It takes us out of healthy relationships.

> Porn normalizes loneliness. It makes isolation
> easy. It takes us out of healthy relationships.

We have seen that our personhood and our sexuality are closely intertwined in our society. If we are not being fulfilled sexually (we are told), something is wrong with us. We are being deprived. Surely this is part of the reason many of our teens are turning to porn.

But what if we proposed something different, something more beautiful? What if we helped kids discover the pleasure of relationships without the sins of lust and porn use? How do we make celibacy plausible?

In his book *Same-Sex Attraction and the Church*, Ed Shaw applies this question to same-sex attraction. He says the church can make the celibate life plausible by providing community, love, and support. By being there through the suffering and struggle. He reminds us that

Jesus lived a celibate life himself and is with our teens in their struggle against lust. We can help our kids understand that through the work of the Spirit and the community of the church, they don't have to give in to their sexual desires. And when they do sin, we are there to help them pick up the pieces.

The Loveliness of Christ

One thing have I asked of the LORD...
to gaze upon the beauty of the LORD
and to inquire in his temple.
PSALM 27:4

It is time for the church to be the church again. It is time for us as fathers and mothers to extend the loveliness of Christ to our children. This is exactly what Thomas Chalmers expounded on so brilliantly in his sermon "The Expulsive Power of a New Affection."[7] He showed that only by loving something more than another thing can we find the power to be rid of the lesser thing.

When our kids love the release and the pleasure they get from porn use, they are loving something less beautiful than authentic relationships with Christ and others. Their lust is focused on themselves and doesn't bring glory to God. But we can show them a better way by helping them to see that Christ and a relationship with him are so much more beautiful than their own sexual fulfillment, pleasure, and disordered desires.

> We can show them a better way by helping them
> to see that Christ and a relationship with him are
> so much more beautiful than their own sexual
> fulfillment, pleasure, and disordered desires.

Self-Control

We also need to replace the porn aesthetic with the beauty of self-control. John A. Younts talks about this in his book *Everyday Talk About Sex and Marriage*.

> The Spirit's fruit of self-control is what counters sensuality. The Holy Spirit's fruit of self-control is not the anguished self-denial of living with unmet desires. Biblical self-control is rooted in the fact that God has better things prepared for his people in sexual relations than we can possibly imagine.[8]

This is the beauty of the fruit of the Spirit. God has so much more to share with us, and we will experience more life as we practice self-control. Let's teach and encourage our teens to practice self-control so they can experience the freedom that comes with saying no to sin.

But here's the rub. Our teens will never know what self-control looks like if they never see it in us. If they only see us maximizing our pleasure, if they don't live in a community where self-control is seen as a beautiful thing, then they will not see self-control as the path to freedom, but to slavery. If we parents are giving in to every desire, our kids will never think they need self-control. Rather, they will believe that life centers around them, and they will give in to their desires.

Dad, if you look at porn, if you are addicted to porn, there is help in Christ. Go to your pastor, your elder, a respected mentor...any mature believer you trust and get help. You cannot expect your son or daughter to reject pornography unless you do. You cannot expect your sons to respect women or to be faithful to their wives if you are being unfaithful and disrespectful by looking at porn. Dear brother in Christ, don't let this pass you by. There are so many resources for you to get help.[9] Utilize them.

But most of all, utilize your community of faith. If you cannot find help in your church, then let me encourage you to go and find help. It will be one of the most difficult things you will ever do, but it is so freeing. The apostle Paul says that "where the Spirit of the Lord is, there is freedom" (2 Corinthians 3:17). This freedom is found only in Christ and the work of his Spirit in you.

I hope you are seeing that we need to live out what we teach our teens. We need to have practical conversations with our kids about how our family members are going to work together to love Jesus more, to see him as more beautiful than our sexual fantasies.

And I hope you are seeing the importance of affirming that humans are made in the image of God. That is why we can love one another and treat one another with care and respect. People who are ensnared in prostitution, trafficking, or pornography bear the image of God. Jesus came to save those people, people who are sinners like you and me. As we talk to our teens about the way they view other people, we need to help them see that even "the least of these" is made in the image of God and deserves respect, love, protection, and care. They deserve not to be used for our own sexual desires.

> As we talk to our teens about the way they view other people, we need to help them see that even "the least of these" is made in the image of God.

Words for Moms

The allurement of another person finding you sexually attractive is a real one, even for us moms. We too have bought into the lie that our worth comes from our ability to control others with our looks. You may be thinking, *Not me. I dress modestly. I don't flaunt anything.* Can I ask you to take a hard look at why you wear what you wear? We may dress modestly to gain respect, or we may dress in unflattering ways to control what others think of us. The truth is that the way we dress, and the reasons behind it, affect our kids. How you dress is up to you and the Holy Spirit. I don't have much to say on the matter, but if the Holy Spirit is convicting you about it, let him speak. Dressing modestly or immodestly does not change our standing with Christ. You are a perfect, holy daughter in his sight.

Let's teach our sons and daughters that women and men are more than bodies. Take advantage of little teaching moments here and there to remind them about this. When the time is right, engage in a more intense talk with them. When your son or daughter makes fun of the way someone looks, use the opportunity to affirm that all people are created in the image of God. At times it seems funny to join in the joking, but those little moments can be used for teaching and training. And for reminding your child that we don't ever judge on the basis of outward appearance.

Bodies aren't shameful. Nakedness isn't shameful. We need to teach that to our children too. But when we use nakedness and bodies for our own pleasure, we don't think of the person we are looking at as someone with a soul. Mom, talk to your boys and girls about what pornography is, why it is dangerous, and how it hurts everyone involved. Bring every conversation back to the love of Christ. Let them know again and again that there is forgiveness. Let them know that no sin is beyond God's grace.

Are you afraid to extend that much grace to them? Sometimes we think we can control our kids through fear. By making them think that if they go too far, they won't recover. That is hogwash. God's grace reaches into the darkest parts of our lives and rescues us. Remind them of that amazing grace and watch it change their lives.

Words for Dads

The porn culture is everywhere. Dad, this is where it hits home for so many of us. We must talk to our teens (our daughters as well as our sons) about how to resist the temptation to look at porn. We need to humanize the people in the images and to teach our teens that these are not just fictional actors, but real people—mothers, daughters, sons, and fathers. We need to challenge our teens to think in these terms. Dad, you may need to learn to think in these terms as well.

We also must show them that lust is the issue that lies behind their porn use. We need to help them understand that when they lust after another human being, they are sinning regardless of whether they act out.

Dad, how can we ask our teens to do something we are unwilling to do? That is a hard question. As we pleaded earlier, if you are addicted to porn, please get help.

In addition to encouraging our kids not to look at pornography, we need to lead them to Christ for forgiveness when they sin. We need to help them find relief from the guilt of their sin. We need to help them understand the depth of their sin and then bring them to Jesus for forgiveness.

Dad, can I ask you if you have gone to Christ with your struggle with lust? Scripture promises that if you go to him and repent of your sins, he will forgive you (Psalm 32; 1 John 1:9). Will you do that now? Will you help your teens do the same?

TALKING POINTS

This is as awkward as awkward gets. We understand that you are afraid of your child encountering pornography, or maybe you are heartbroken with the knowledge that they already have. Here are some talking points to help get the conversation going.

- Understand that the over-sexualization of society is everywhere. Don't be surprised by it.

- Talk to your children about the importance of seeing everyone as an image bearer of God. People are not to be used for our own pleasure. They are more than just a body. Each person has a soul.

- Talk to them about the dangers of porn—for those involved and for those who watch.

- Make sure your kids know they can talk to you if they have viewed porn or they have an addiction to porn. Create a culture of grace. Give them an opportunity to ask for help.

- Remember that only love for Christ can change a person's heart. Give them the good news of forgiveness and redemption.

Part 3

How to Have Great Conversations About Sex

8

Soul Building Instead of Soul Crushing

The Gospel and Sex

I appeal to you therefore, brothers, by the mercies of God, to present your bodies as a living sacrifice, holy and acceptable to God, which is your spiritual worship. Do not be conformed to this world, but be transformed by the renewal of your mind, that by testing you may discern what is the will of God, what is good and acceptable and perfect.

ROMANS 12:1-2

When we talk with our kids about sexuality, we don't want to sound like dorks. We want to sound informed and hip, understanding but firm in our convictions that what the Bible says about sexuality is true and lasting. We don't want to be hypocrites, and we certainly don't want to lose our kids.

So how do we talk with them about these topics in a way that builds them up, is understanding, and gives them hope? How do we display the beauty of the gospel? Being biblical and being relevant are not mutually exclusive. How do we do both? In short, we want to build their souls instead of crushing them.

What do we mean by soul building? We want to propose a way of talking with our kids about sexuality that holds out the beauty of sex and the beauty of the gospel in such a way that our kids hear more than "Avoid sex at all costs." We want to acknowledge the reality that no one expects them to be perfect (only Jesus is) and that there is hope for people who fail.

Every single one of us fails and will continue to fail until we are home with Christ. Every single one of us is in desperate need of something outside us to make a relationship with God possible. We all need hope. This hope is found in the reconciling work of Christ for us, which gives us the motivation to follow God's desires for us sexually. This is soul building.

Sex Is Not a Problem to Be Solved

Sometimes I feel as if the only times my kids and I talk about sex is when they say or do something wrong. We do this because sex is an uncomfortable topic and we don't want to address it until we absolutely have to. We also feel ill-equipped or perhaps guilty about our own sexual past.

But there is a danger in discussing sex with your kids only when something is not the way you want it to be. When that is the only time we talk about sex, we put sex in a negative light. We treat it as a problem to be solved, a disease to be avoided, and we take the beauty out of sex. God gave sex to humanity as a good gift, not as a curse. Sex was given as a picture of a love that is beautiful, not problematic. But if we talk with our teens about sex only when we catch them doing something we don't approve of, sex is no longer beautiful—it's a disciplinable offense.

God gave sex to humanity as a good gift, not as a curse.

How do we break this cycle, and how do we help our kids think about sex in a healthy way when they do struggle? Let me propose to you two scenarios. In one, we'll see how a father and his daughter can talk about sex in a normal, ongoing conversation. In the other, we'll see how to talk when things blow up.

Soul Building Through Normal Conversations

Teach them diligently to your children, and...
talk of them when you sit in your house.

Deuteronomy 6:7

A dad takes his daughter out for breakfast. He has no agenda; he just wants to be in touch with her and her struggles. On this daddy date, he asks good questions about life and just listens. He doesn't try to steer the conversation. He orders coffee and then says, "So how is life?" This simple question starts a new way of life for his relationship with his daughter.

He does this again on another date to the ice cream parlor and then again on a shopping date. He spends time building a relationship of trust and understanding. He shows her that he wants to know *her*, not just whether she is obeying the family rules. He asks about her wants, dreams, and desires. He asks about the pressures she faces every day. Every time they go out, he sets the expectation that they will talk about various facets of life.

A few months into these daddy dates, he asks, "Is it okay if we start to have an open dialogue about the goodness of sex? I know it's kind of awkward, and I'll try not to use any cheesy illustrations. And you can stop the conversation if it gets weird. But I think you're old enough to handle this kind of conversation. What do you think?"

She says, "Umm, okay..."

"Good. Are you okay with us having these conversations over coffee or dessert or wherever we can find somewhere private but still have some good food?"

"Sure."

"Great. Are you okay with us starting tonight? I want to respect your time and ability to concentrate. I know this is awkward—it is for me as well—but we may as well get started. God has given us such a good gift in sex. Let's open up our Bibles to Genesis 1."

"Dad, I didn't bring my Bible."

"That's okay, 'cause I did. I am kinda sneaky like that."

In this scenario, Dad is taking some big risks. His daughter could say no, and he needs to respect that. His daughter may feel more comfortable talking to her mother. Either way, both Dad and Mom need to have ongoing dialogues with their children to help them understand God, the world, and how they fit in. It is the parents' privilege to help their kids with that understanding.

> Both Dad and Mom need to have ongoing dialogues with their children to help them understand God, the world, and how they fit in.

Deuteronomy 6:4-9 helps us understand this concept. God has just had his dad talk with Moses (and Israel by extension), and now Moses is declaring that word to Israel. Moses tells them about who God is and how they are to respond in love to that truth.[1] Then Moses says this:

> Hear, O Israel: The LORD our God, the LORD is one. You shall love the LORD your God with all your heart and with all your soul and with all your might. And these words that I command you today shall be on your heart. You shall teach them diligently to your children, and shall talk of them when you sit in your house, and when you walk by the way, and when you lie down, and when you rise. You shall bind them as a sign on your hand, and they shall be as frontlets between your eyes. You shall write them on the doorposts of your house and on your gates.

Moses is describing a way of life, not a singular event. He says that wherever we go, whatever we talk about, God is an important part of the discussion. There is no part of our lives that God does not transform. The beauty of the gospel makes God our Father. It is our privilege as parents to hold out these truths to our teens.

So, how do we talk to our teens about sex? Begin to have conversations with them. In normal contexts and in normal ways. Treat sex just like any other subject. When we make sex weird or gross or wrong, our kids will have a skewed view of sex. Instead, let's take the awkwardness out of the conversation and show our kids the beauty of sex in normal conversations.

> Begin to have conversations with them. In normal contexts and in normal ways. Treat sex just like any other subject.

Soul Building in Times of Sin and Sadness

Be gracious to me, O God, according to Your lovingkindness.

PSALM 51:1 NASB

A 16-year-old boy is caught looking at pornography. His mother found the image searches on his computer in the internet history. She calls his father. They both weep. Scared, they have a sinking feeling in the pit of their stomachs. They had noticed that their son had been acting strange lately—hiding things, sullen, big mood swings. What do they do? Mom is afraid he is a sexual deviant. Dad is angry he did this to Mom, although Dad has been hiding his pornography addiction as well. Dad feels the guilt and the shame. Their son doesn't know that they know yet.

"We need to talk to him," Mom says. "I was afraid this would happen. Where did we go wrong? We have been there for him, but I knew that not having internet filters was a mistake. I told you to put them on the devices."

Dad, seething with anger and racked with shame, replies, "I know. I'm so sorry you found those image searches. I will take care of it when I get home."

Now fill in the blanks. What would you do? What have you done? This is typically when I (Joel) get a phone call from the parents. Why? Because most parents don't know what to say in these instances. They love their children, and they don't want to lose them. They are angry, sad, hurt, and lost.

What do you say? How do you handle your child's sexual sin? In some ways it depends on the child and where they are. We parents often miss this. We need to ask some questions about our kids before we start talking. Is my child saved? Are they feeling shame and guilt? Are they being arrogant? Are they being rebellious? Is this a pattern? Is this defiance?

We also need to ask some questions about ourselves. How am I responding to this—with anger? Shame? Frustration? Do I care more about my own reputation than the soul of my child? These are tough questions that expose more about who we are and what we think than we would like.

Psalm 51 is a great psalm of David in which he reflects on his affair with Bathsheba and his murder of her husband, Uriah. Let me encourage you to open your Bible and read it right now.

When David reflects on his sin, he repents to God first because his sin is primarily against God. In one sense this is terrifying, but in another sense it is freeing. It is terrifying because when our children sin sexually, they break God's law. It is freeing because we don't have to take their sin personally.

> When David reflects on his sin, he repents to God
> first because his sin is primarily against God.

David begins this psalm by crying out to God for mercy, and he finds that mercy in God's steadfast covenant love for his people. What is so reassuring about God is that when he makes a covenant with his people, he always keeps his covenant. David approaches him on the basis of this hope and confesses his sin.

Yes, our kids have broken our rules. Yes, that is bad. Yes, they need to be disciplined for breaking the rules. But if the God of the universe can forgive their sins, we can as well.

So, how do we respond to this or any other discussion concerning sex with our kids? Is our primary motivation for them to fall in love with Christ? Or just to not have sex? Are these two things mutually exclusive? No! So how do we talk to our kids about sex and sexuality, honestly answering their questions, encouraging them toward a view of the beauty of sex in its proper context without crushing their souls?

The Gospel Is the Point, Not Sexual Purity

Wait, what? Did I just write that? Yes, I did. We can teach our kids about the beauty of sex. Here's why.

In Romans 11, the apostle Paul describes the beauty of our salvation and God's work of predestination. The chapter ends with him breaking out in a song of praise. The next chapter begins with these words: "I appeal to you therefore, brothers, by the mercies of God, to present your bodies as a living sacrifice, holy and acceptable to God, which is your spiritual worship."

This should give us a clue as to what he considers the reason for our purity. When Paul says "therefore," we need to understand that he is making the logical conclusion to the arguments he has been advancing all along. It is like saying, "Now that I have told you about the gospel, here's the proper response."

Paul has already used the word "present" in Romans 6:13: "Do not present your members to sin as instruments for unrighteousness, but present yourselves to God as those who have been brought from death to life, and your members to God as instruments for righteousness." Paul is not saying, "Do not present your members to sin, or God will no longer love you." He's not saying, "God will be very disappointed in you." If he did say that, the pressure would be on us, and our motivation to obey would be based on fear. Instead he says, "Don't present your bodies as instruments of sin, because Christ has resurrected you." Paul uses the word "present" in verses 16 and 19 in connection with this idea.

Paul wants us to know that what we do is intimately connected with our understanding of the gospel. This gospel affects our whole person, inside and out—this is what he means by presenting our bodies. Our sexuality is only one part of us, and to limit the gospel's work to that one part is to undercut the power of the good news.

On the other hand, if we tell our kids that the gospel is only for our spiritual need and the rest of life is up to us, we make keeping the commands of God a hopeless burden. Why? Because Jesus's commands are never just about outward obedience (Mark 10:17-27). They place requirements on our entire being. This is why we need to be sure to keep the gospel at the center of all our conversations with our kids about sex.

If merely abstaining from sex (a huge feat in itself) were good enough, then anyone who does that would be able to say, "I kept the law, God, now give me my due!" But Jesus deepens the command and says, "But I say to you that everyone who looks at a woman with lustful intent has already committed adultery with her in his heart" (Matthew 5:28). No one escapes from this—all of us have sinned in our hearts in one way or another. We need the only news with the power to change us down to our hearts, to take away even the sins that we commit in our hearts. We need the gospel.

The gospel is the reconciling work of Christ. It is the only thing that brings about freedom from guilt and shame of sexual sin in thought or deed. That is why it is the first thing we talk about with our kids when it comes to their sexuality. What makes you love God more than you love sex? The gospel. It is the only thing powerful enough to do that.

In a situation like the one described above, parents can share the gospel with their kids by echoing the apostle Paul: "Christ Jesus came into the world to save sinners, of whom I am the foremost" (1 Timothy 1:15). Let them hear you say that. Too often we make divisions—parents versus kids, good kids versus disobedient kids—instead of celebrating our unity. We are brothers and sisters in Christ running together to our Savior.

Admit to your kids that you are a sinner just like they are. This will help you avoid trying to shame them into better behavior. Create a habit of confession and repentance in your house, and it will be easier for children to confess and repent when they fall into sin. If this is new to you, an easy way to start confessing is to say something like, "I sinned against you and against God by believing that [name the sin] was better than Jesus."

May our parental hearts beat with the message that Jesus is better than our sin. May our kids hear from our lips that we long for them to be rooted and grounded in Christ's love for them. May we, by the work of the Holy Spirit, build in them such a magnificent picture of Jesus's love that they will not go anywhere else for satisfaction. May our prayer echo Paul's in Ephesians 3:18-19: "May [you] have strength to comprehend with all the saints what is the breadth and length and height and depth, and to know the love of Christ that surpasses knowledge, that you may be filled with all the fullness of God." Let's gush over his great love and faithfulness to hardened sinners and let that theme ring in our households.

> May our parental hearts beat with
> the message that Jesus is better than our sin.

Jesus Christ himself said that he didn't come for those who think they have it all together, but for the sick. He loved the immoral ones, he broke bread with the unfaithful ones—and thank God for that, or none of us could sit at his table. The church has often gotten it all wrong. We've silenced and ousted the sexually immoral when Jesus spoke peace and forgiveness to them. Is this the Jesus your children know? If it is, they will be free to repent, they will desire to live in the light of the gospel, and they will be compelled to be obedient because of his love.

By all means, talk to your children about the insidious nature of pornography. Explain to them that those aren't objects they are looking at—they are image bearers. Tell them that viewing pornography isn't just a private sin; it affects people who may be held as sex slaves or addicted to drugs or just plain lost. Tell them all those things. Have the conversation with your kids no matter how uncomfortable.

But please couch all this in the forgiveness of sins available for those who are in Christ Jesus. Make sure they hear that "neither death nor life nor viewing porn nor things present nor things to come will separate them from the love of God in Christ." Give them hope for change. Give them something better. Give them Jesus Christ.

Restoration Is the Point

If anyone is caught in any transgression...
restore him in a spirit of gentleness.
GALATIANS 6:1

So often when our kids sin sexually, the last thing we think about is restoration. We think about the shame their sin will bring on everybody. We feel sad, betrayed, and angry. Our hearts are broken. When we discover the website searches, when we get the phone call from another parent, or however the news comes to us, we are not usually focused on restoration and peace. Instead, we want to make it hurt.

Sin breaks communion. Sin creates distance. When our children sin, they become disconnected, and they need their relationships with God and with us to be restored. God continues to love them, and if they are Christians, their position with God does not change. But if they continue in their sin, God turns his blessing away from them as a way to draw them to repentance.[2]

When the Bible speaks about discipline, it places the emphasis on restoration (Galatians 6:1). Restoration is the point.

Some may object, "Does this mean we don't discipline our kids? Or make it hurt?"

If your ultimate goal in discipline is to restore them or even to break them so they can be restored, then yes, by all means discipline them. But if your purpose is solely to make a point or have them learn a lesson without restoration, you are on shaky ground biblically.

Take out your Bible and read Matthew 18:10-35 even if it is super familiar. We've all been taught that the most important rule of interpretation is that context is king. We need to read everything in its context, and if we ignore the context of a passage, we are very likely to misread the text.

This passage includes the parable of the lost sheep, Jesus's teaching on confrontation, and the parable of the unforgiving servant. Let's start with an overview of these three parts. What are they all about? Forgiveness and restoration!

In the parable of the lost sheep, a man owns a hundred sheep and one of them runs away. What does this signify? The one sheep who leaves represents a human who runs from Christ in his sinfulness. (This does not have to be an unbeliever.) Jesus then asks an insightful question: Will the owner leave the ninety-nine to save the one and restore it to the flock? Think about what this would mean—danger from predators and thieves. And, because sheep are not the brightest of animals, they need to be led to places to eat and drink. But this owner leaves his sheep to fend for themselves and feed themselves.

Now, notice the way the owner reacts when he finds the one sheep. He rejoices over it more than he rejoices over the ninety-nine who did not bail. Those are tough words for us when we think about the way we react when we find our children in sin. Do we seek to restore our kids to Christ and to the family? Do we rejoice over the ones who are restored, or do we see them as a nuisance? Notice this restoration is the will of the Father in heaven (2 Peter 3:9).

After sharing this parable, Jesus explains what it means by teaching about restoration. He begins by saying, "When your brother sins against you..." Notice a few things about this statement. First, the person who sins is our brother. He is not referring to familial connections. Rather, all who walk with Christ are brothers and sisters in him. So we have a dual relationship with our children—they are not only our kids but also our brothers or sisters.

Jesus calls us to work hard at restoration. Confrontation is not the hard part; restoration is. When we seek to restore our children, we need to keep the parable of the lost sheep in mind. God has sought you and me out and restored us to be his people. This is all of grace. In fact, we don't deserve to be restored; we deserve to be left to the lions. Grace motivates us to be restored and to restore. If this is what God has done for us, then it should inform the way we work with our kids.

> Jesus calls us to work hard at restoration.
> Confrontation is not the hard part; restoration is.

Peter has been listening to Jesus explain all of this, and his mind is blown, so he asks the question that is running through our minds: How many times do we have to forgive in this manner? You can't be serious, Jesus. Don't you know what my kids have done? Don't you understand the seriousness of their sin?

Jesus replies with the parable of the unforgiving servant. He says that a servant owes his master a ton of money, and the master forgives the debt. The forgiven servant then turns to another servant who owes him a significant amount of money but nothing close to the amount the first servant owed. The second servant doesn't have the money, so the first servant strangles him and sends him to jail. When the master hears of it he says, "I forgave you all that debt because you pleaded with me. And should not you have had mercy on your fellow servant, as I had mercy on you?" (Matthew 18:32-33). What is the point? The point is, when we have been forgiven and restored, that should produce in us a heart of forgiveness and a desire to restore others.

We read about restoration throughout the New Testament. When God disciplines, he does so out of love (Hebrews 12:3-11). When we look at the Old Testament, we see the same thing. God disciplines Israel, but always with his mind set on restoration. The punishment of exile is tied to the promise of restoration (Deuteronomy 30:1-10).

So is there a place for the law? Is there a place for us to say, "This is how we honor God with our bodies"?

The Use of the Law

What do we do about the law? Is there a place for instruction that holds the law of God as the norm for our sexual conduct? Yes, of course there is. So much of the testimony of Scripture tells us this.

The law of the Lord is perfect, reviving the soul; the testimony of the Lord is sure, making wise the simple; the precepts of the Lord are right, rejoicing the heart; the commandment of the Lord is pure, enlightening the eyes; the fear of the Lord is clean, enduring forever; the rules of the Lord are true, and righteous altogether. More to be desired are they than gold, even much fine gold; sweeter also than honey and drippings of the honeycomb. Moreover, by them is your servant warned; in keeping them there is great reward. Who can discern his errors? Declare me innocent from hidden faults. Keep back your servant also from presumptuous sins; let them not have dominion over me! Then I shall be blameless, and innocent of great transgression. Let the words of my mouth and the meditation of my heart be acceptable in your sight, O Lord, my rock and my redeemer (Psalm 19:7-14).

The apostle Paul picks up on this in Romans 7, where he says that the law of the Lord is pure and holy. As we saw in the first part of this book, it is vital for us to have a biblically informed view of sex. So yes, you should teach your child God's commands concerning their sexuality. But it is here that we must say that we need to use the law properly. The law is kind of like the crane kick from *Karate Kid*—when done rightly, none can defend. John Calvin said that there are three uses to the law:

1. It is a mirror that reflects to us God's perfect holiness and our sinfulness. This use exposes our sin and drives us to Christ.

2. It restrains evil. This is often referred to as the civil use of the law. This use helps to norm societal standards.

3. It is a guide for the regenerate. This use helps provide a roadmap to our lives.[3]

The law is good; without the law we cannot know what God expects of us. Without the law we don't know and cannot know how we should act sexually. The law has so much to say in this area. It instructs us to not have sex until marriage. It tells us that adultery is a sin. It says that pornography and lust are sinful. The law says that homosexuality is a sin. The law instructs us that sex with anyone to whom you are not married is sinful. Incest is sinful. Bestiality is sinful. Sexual assault and sexual harassment are sinful.

We know that in saying this we have now crossed a line and moved into an area that makes all of us uncomfortable. But if Calvin is correct about his first use of the law, then without knowing the law we have no way of knowing we need a Savior! Also, in naming all these things as sinful, we are not separating ourselves into two groups—people who struggle with these sins and people who don't. Rather, all of us are in the same boat. First John 1:10 says, "If we say we have not sinned, we make him a liar, and his word is not in us." If we make the law something that divides us from those around us, setting up a distinction between our kids (who have sinned) and ourselves (who have not sinned), we alienate and crush them. But if we take Matthew 5:28 seriously and admit that lust is just as much a sin as adultery is, we can identify with the sin in our kids' hearts. We can approach them with humility and a desire to see them restored to Christ. This is how we apply the law lovingly and gently to our believing children and move them to Christ. And it's how we move *with* them toward Christ as we confess our own sin, especially if we have responded to our kids inappropriately.

This is the winsome nature of the gospel. Jesus was about soul building instead of soul crushing. Of course, if your child is not a believer in Christ, they need to hear how they, like you, can never meet the requirements of God's law, and that is the reason why they need Jesus. Their good works will never get them into heaven. Their good works done outside of Christ are nothing, but in Christ they are God honoring.

> Their good works done outside of Christ are nothing, but in Christ they are God honoring.

When we crush our believing children with the law, the result is often a downward spiral of sin compounded by sin. Soul crushing leads to hiding (see Psalm 32). If our kids are afraid that God is not for them, but is against them, they will hide. This broken communion, this unhealthy fear of God, does not lead to loving obedience out of gratitude for what God has done for them in Christ. It may curb their sin for a while (which is not a bad thing), but it will not replace their idol of sexual fulfillment with the true satisfaction of being loved by God at a level that meets their needs.

When I (Joel) was growing up, I was always afraid of God even though I was a Christian. (I committed myself to Christ five or six times as a teen!) I thought God hated me and found me dirty. This led me to search for satisfaction in so many sins, which led to more self-loathing, which led to more sin…until I finally gave up trying to please God. Even though I went to church every Sunday, I felt like the black sheep of the church. I could not come to God and find forgiveness because I wasn't convinced he would forgive me. My soul was crushed.

To be sure, this was not my parents' or my pastor's intention, but it was my interpretation of what I was hearing over and over again. Then one night, after being confronted with my sin once again, I called Ruth (we weren't married yet). We prayed together for God to forgive me, and I finally felt the freedom I had always hoped I could have. This new reality actually gave me the hope I needed to fight my sin.

Hope at Midnight

I came not to call the righteous, but sinners.
MARK 2:17

As I read the Gospels, I am more and more struck by the way Jesus acts in such unexpected ways. This is what makes him so awesome. When we expect him to heal the paralytic, he forgives his sins without the paralytic even asking! And then he heals his legs too (Mark 2:1-12)! When we expect Jesus to tell the prostitute and the tax collector—notorious sinners—to leave him so he can chill with the powerful, Jesus instead says, "Those who are well have no need of a physician, but those who are sick. I came not to call the righteous, but sinners" (Mark 2:17). It is precisely the people who sin sexually whom Jesus comes to save.

It is precisely the people who sin sexually whom Jesus comes to save.

This is the best news ever for your son or daughter who has just gotten caught. It is the best news ever for you and your spouse when you face an unexpected teen pregnancy. Jesus cares for and loves broken people. Let this message of hope fill your heart and your conversations with your teens. God doesn't accept their sin, but he doesn't expect perfection either. Mind blown. Praise God!

Words for Moms

When our hearts get broken as mothers because our kids have sinned sexually, we can have a number of different reactions. We can blame ourselves for not being present enough and for not talking to them enough about the gospel or our family's rules or just normal everyday life. This path will lead to depression. We can blame our spouse, especially if the child is the same sex as they are. We can wonder why they weren't more involved. We can blame outside circumstances, a divorce, a bully at school, a friend who was a bad influence, a youth pastor who wasn't interested enough…on and on the list can go. We can just blame the kid, figuring something is wrong with them.

We are always looking for a place to lay the blame. We think that if we can find someone to blame, we will somehow be able to solve the problem. Trying to solve our kids as if they were a problem (yes, that reminds me of *The Sound of Music*) will crush their souls. Can I encourage you to try a different path? Instead of looking to blame someone and then fix a problem, try taking that brokenness to Jesus. Take your brokenness, your child's brokenness, your spouse's brokenness to the Great Healer. Let him use whatever horrible situation has presented itself in your family's life to draw you all closer to each other and to him.

Doing that with our kids will be soul building. Build in them a full and beautiful picture of God's grace. Let them know that he forgives every sin—yes, even *that* sin. Let them know that God's grace is bigger than all our sin. Stand *with* your child in their brokenness instead of against them. I understand that you may be experiencing great feelings of hurt, but they are sinners just like you are. Treat them as fellow sinners in need of a strong Savior.

Words for Dads

Dad, this is one of the most difficult parts of this book for us. We deal with issues all day long, and many of us do best when we are able to lay down the law. But this is one of those areas where patient, loving instruction pays off. Why? Because we are fighting a war with a system that wants us to be impatient so that it can patiently move in and explain why things should be viewed differently. Our kids need us to walk with them and provide them with a worldview that makes sense of God's revelation.

I know that it's difficult. I understand that we all are busy and tired. I get it that talking to our teens about sex is not what we want to do when we get home from a long day at work. But this is one of the most important things we do as fathers because it imitates our heavenly Father.

TALKING POINTS

This might be a time to refrain from telling your kids anything. Instead, ask questions and listen. Here are some talking points to help get the conversation going.

- Ask your child what they have learned from you about sex.

- Ask if they have any questions about sex.

- Ask if they feel like they could talk to you about sex.

- Ask if they feel like sex is a good thing or a bad thing.

- Ask if they think that if they messed up they could come to you and tell you about what they have done.

- Ask if they think sexual sins are worse than other sins.

9

Help and Hope for Parents
The Gospel and You

Since we have confidence to enter the holy places by the blood of Jesus, by the new and living way that he opened for us through the curtain, that is, through his flesh, and since we have a great priest over the house of God, let us draw near with a true heart in full assurance of faith, with our hearts sprinkled clean from an evil conscience and our bodies washed with pure water.

HEBREWS 10:19–22

Parenting is a series of moments in a series of days in a series of weeks in a series of months in a series of years in which you feel completely ill-equipped. Some of these moments, days, weeks, months, and years are sweet, and you may feel as if you are actually getting the hang of it all. Then you are confronted with a moment that completely derails you. You are hit smack upside the head by reality. You are reminded of your lack of knowledge, your lack of patience, your lack of connection with your child. Those brutal reminders may leave you feeling hopeless, helpless, and wondering if you should just give up.

I (Jessica) have felt this sinking hopelessness and helplessness on several occasions throughout my 18 years of parenting. I have made huge mistakes. I have purposefully hurt my kids. I have been distant. I have been angry. I have been ignorant. I have been lazy. I have just been flat-out wrong. Especially on the topic of educating my kids about sex, I have been absent and have ignored my duties as a mother. I have to admit to being convicted more than once while writing this book. I have let myself sink into the "I should have done better" quicksand. Instead of deciding to fix it, I have actually had the thought, *Well, they are almost out of the house. I mean, why have the conversation now?*

My oldest son is sitting next to me right now as I type this. He looked over, read what I wrote, and said, "Yep. That's true. You sorta left us hanging in the wind on that one." I wish I could tell you I have set a better example.

But let me just say that since the inception of this book, things have changed around our house. By the help of the Holy Spirit, I have said no to those thoughts and to that quicksand and have been able to have many good conversations with my kids. Most of those talks started awkwardly, but now the conversations are easier to have. I started having in-depth conversations about sex with my daughter when she was in third grade, but I didn't do that with my boys until more recently. I promise that it will get easier. The more you pursue them and pursue conversations with them about sex, the easier starting that conversation will become.

Missed Opportunities

Regret is a parent's constant companion. I have regretted the conversations I didn't have. I have regretted the conversations I did have but screwed up. I regret not being able to have all the answers. I regret having the wrong answers and thinking they were right. I have allowed my kids to learn about sex from sources I shouldn't have allowed into their lives.

As I get older, I am becoming less adamant about a few issues and seeing the need for more grace. And some of the issues that I thought were not all that important are now on the top of my list. I learn. I adapt. I have an adult son, and I am still trying to figure this thing out.

All this would be really depressing if it were all up to me or up to my spouse to make sure that our kids turned out perfectly. But, brother or sister, it isn't all up to us. We have hope. Missed opportunities don't define us. Ignored opportunities don't define us. Something bigger than our mistakes can inform the way our kids turn out.

All this would be really depressing if it were all up to me or up to my spouse to make sure that our kids turned out perfectly.

Our Hope

It is by grace you have been saved through faith.

EPHESIANS 2:8 NIV

Our only hope in this immense job of parenting is that our kids' salvation does not depend on us getting it right. Our hope rests solely, completely, and wholly on the grace of God. "By grace you have been saved through faith. And this is not your own doing; it is the gift of God, not a result of works, so that no one can boast" (Ephesians 2:8-9).

Our hope rests on our God, who saves sinners. "Here is a trustworthy saying that deserves full acceptance: Christ Jesus came into the world to save sinners, of whom I am the worst" (1 Timothy 1:15 NIV).

Our hope rests on our God, who reconciles enemies to himself. "If while we were enemies we were reconciled to God by the death of his Son, much more, now that we are reconciled, shall we be saved by his life" (Romans 5:10).

Our hope rests on our God, who loves sinners. "God shows his love for us that while we were still sinners, Christ died for us" (Romans 5:8).

Our hope rests on our God, who lavishes mercy on the undeserving. "When the goodness and loving kindness of God our Savior appeared, he saved us, not because of works done by us in righteousness, but according to his own mercy" (Titus 3:4-5).

Our hope rests on our God, who is able to save to the uttermost. "He is able to save to the uttermost those who draw near to God through him, since he always lives to make intercession for them" (Hebrews 7:25).

But God

Salvation belongs to the LORD!
JONAH 2:9

Our hope isn't in ourselves. Our hope isn't in our ability to get *the talk* just right. Our hope is in a God who can and does use any means necessary to make a family out of rebels. We will screw up *the talk*. Our emotions, our past history, our biases, our flawed thinking...these things and more will get in the way of what is biblical and true. *But God*—he used Moses to be his mouthpiece when Moses was sure he couldn't do it. Moses was sure he would say the wrong things in the wrong way, *but God* used him anyway. Moses wasn't just having a sex talk with his kids; he was telling Pharaoh, the leader of the country, to release all his slaves. I'm pretty sure if God can use Moses, he can use us as well. Moses was sure he couldn't do it, *but God* will use us according to his plan.

> Our hope is in a God who can and does use any means necessary to make a family out of rebels.

As I travel the country and speak at parenting conferences, the number one concern I hear from parents over and over again is that they think they aren't doing it right. They are stressing over their kids' food choices, screen time, discipline, church attendance, and friends. But primarily they are concerned about their children's salvation and their own inability to communicate the gospel in a way that their children will understand.

Over and over again, I have told parents what I want to tell you: Your child's salvation does not rest on your ability to communicate the gospel in a clear way. Your child's salvation rests on a good heavenly Father who rejoices in making his name great. Your kids' salvation is not your cross to bear. That should take a lot of pressure off when you talk to them about sex or about God or about their day. You will make mistakes. You will communicate in a broken way. *But God* isn't thwarted by your mess-ups. He isn't stopped by your laziness. He actually even uses your sins to bring about his own glory.

So don't give up even if you feel as if it's too late. Even if you feel as if you've already said everything wrong, even if you don't think your kids will ever listen to you, don't give up. We have a Father who turns hopeless situations into beautiful displays of his glory. Look at the cross. The disciples thought it was over. The bad guys had won. Their only hope was dead. *But God* raised Jesus from the dead. He can do the same for you regardless of what your family situation looks like.

Hope for Your Own Sexual Brokenness

We trust you are finding hope that you can communicate truths about sex to your children—finding hope that he will use your screwups when you talk with your kids.

We also want you to find hope that God can heal your pain from your sexual past. He promises forgiveness regardless of your sexual history. All of us experience this in part now, but one day you will experience complete healing. You don't have to be defined by what happened to you. You are now an adopted, forgiven, pure, and loved child of the King. You don't have to be defined by what you have done.

This does not mean we won't experience consequences. We will still experience pain. We still have memories. But we don't have to be enslaved to the pain and memories. Instead, we can bring them to our Father, who loves us and cares about us and forgives us. He sees our broken hearts. He is near to us. He sympathizes with us. He doesn't just leave us to figure out the consequences of our sin. He prays for us. He feels our pain. He doesn't just tell us to get over it. He touches us with healing. He loves us. We have this promise from 2 Corinthians 1:3-5:

> Blessed be the God and Father of our Lord Jesus Christ, the
> Father of mercies and God of all comfort, who comforts us

in all our affliction, so that we may be able to comfort those who are in any affliction, with the comfort with which we ourselves are comforted by God. For as we share abundantly in Christ's sufferings, so through Christ we share abundantly in comfort too.

We have all experienced tragedies and heartache, *but God* can use them to help our children. Nothing is wasted. Even in your most horrific situation, God can comfort you and help you to better understand and comfort your children.

> Even in your most horrific situation, God can comfort you and help you to better understand and comfort your children.

Help for Parents

The pressure is off. You don't have to get the parenting thing just right. Just open the door for open communication. You have the Holy Spirit to help you and guide you. Take a moment to reread that last sentence, and let that truth sink deep into your heart. In fact, now might be a good time to tell God about your concern and to ask him for his help and guidance.

Sometimes when I (Jessica) am about to have a potentially difficult conversation with my kids, I feel a bit out of control, like a flag on top of a hill, flapping around in the wind. Nothing of substance is near that flag—just rocks and some shrubs. The only constant is that the wind can't make up its mind which way it wants to blow. The scene feels desolate, confusing, lonely. I don't know whether you've experienced the same sort of feeling, but I'm sure there are times you feel ill-equipped. Otherwise, you wouldn't have picked up this book.

This feeling can produce a few different responses from me. Sometimes I get angry. Angry at whom? I am not quite sure—maybe everyone—but I feel anger rising in me when I'm asked a question I can't answer or that may lead to a difficult conversation. I'm angry at myself for not knowing how to respond. I'm angry at my kids for asking questions. I'm angry at my spouse for not always being next to me with the right answer. I'm angry at my parents for not teaching me about this topic. I'm angry at the dog for shedding. I'm angry that the music I'm listening to is so loud I can't think.

I'm angry at anyone and anything that takes my mind off the fact that I have weakness, that my mind isn't what it should be. That regardless of what I tell my kids, I actually don't know everything. This anger is a result of my pride. Sometimes I think I have it all together, but at least once a day I am confronted with the fact that I actually don't.

Other times when I'm asked a question I don't know how to answer, I feel sad and depressed. I get really down on myself. I think about all the time I wasted watching *Stranger Things* again on Netflix, or I think about all the hours I spent watching the Padres lose again. My mind goes from activity to activity, and I wonder why I didn't spend that time studying or getting smarter. Sometimes I feel sad because I have studied a subject but can't remember what other smart people have said or what I learned. That sends me into a series of depressing thoughts, including *I am the worst*. This too is a function of my pride. I really think I should be a better, smarter parent than I am.

How do you react when you are faced with a difficult conversation? Do you ever get loud and authoritative and power through, hoping your kids won't see your weakness or lack of knowledge? Do you ever ignore your child's questions and just move on to something else, hoping they won't bring them up again?

And on occasion, do you actually stop and pray? Are you sometimes able to remember that the Holy Spirit lives in you, and his job is to help, guide, and direct you? The same Holy Spirit who gave you life has the power to draw your children too. He can use every one of our bumbling attempts to be good parents as he does his beautiful work in our lives and our kids' lives.

Our Help

I can do all things through him who strengthens me.

Philippians 4:13

Our greatest resource isn't a list of snappy sayings or a collection of profound truths to remember. Rather, our best help is the third person of the Trinity, God himself. In Philippians 4:13, Paul shows us how to admit our weakness and rely on our Savior for everything. "I can do all things through him who strengthens me." This verse is often used to tell us that we are capable, we are strong, we are able to conquer anything. We tend to focus on the first five words. But actually, this is not a battle cry of strength—it's an admittance of weakness. The key truth of the verse is the last five words. Paul is screaming from the mountaintops that it isn't his own strength that gets him through the times of hunger or need or stress. Rather, it is God's strength that sustains him.

We must be able to say the exact same thing in our parenting: "I can do this because of Christ." Not because you've read all the right books, not because you discipline just right, not because you are the cool parent. You can do this because he is with you and promises to give you the strength you need. So join Paul in admitting your weakness and running to your Savior.

In John 14, Jesus tells his disciples he is about to leave them. Understandably, they panic—Thomas asks for clearer directions, Philip asks for more proof, and Peter assures Jesus that he's got serious faith in him. Jesus sees through all of that and tells them the Holy Spirit is going to be there after he leaves.

> I will ask the Father, and he will give you another Helper, to be with you forever, even the Spirit of truth, whom the world cannot receive, because it neither sees him nor knows him. You know him, for he dwells with you and will be in you (verses 16-17).

You have a Helper. You aren't a flag on a lonely mountain, flapping in the wind. You have the Holy Spirit, and he is with you forever. He is your Helper in moments when you don't know what to say. He is your Helper in moments when you *do* know what to say but say it the wrong way. He is your Helper when your own sexual brokenness or experiences are stopping you from sharing the truth with your kids. He dwells with you and is in you. He helps you with the big conversations and the small conversations. He is always and forever your help. Don't think the topic is too small to ask for his help. He is there for you.

Immanuel, God with us, is your Savior's name. You don't ever have to feel as if you are doing this parenting gig all by yourself. God sent Jesus so we would always know he is with us and he is for us. You don't have to figure it all out by yourself. You don't have to run from this method to that method, trying to get it just right. Instead, whenever you feel attacked, you can take Isaiah 30:15-17 to heart.

> For thus said the Lord GOD, the Holy One of Israel, "In returning and rest you shall be saved; in quietness and in trust shall be your strength." But you were unwilling, and you said, "No! We will flee upon horses"; therefore you shall flee away; and, "We will ride upon swift steeds"; therefore your pursuers shall be swift. A thousand shall flee at the threat of one; at the threat of five you shall flee, till you are left like a flagstaff on the top of a mountain, like a signal on a hill.

In quietness, in returning, in rest, in trust…that is where our salvation comes from. Yes, it is good to be educated and to know what you think and why you think it. It is good to share that information with your kids. But ultimately the rest, salvation, and quietness you long for come only from trusting in the Lord God. When you feel like that flag on top of the hill, flapping around aimlessly, consider whether you are trusting in your own methods or trusting in God. Then take your concerns and cares to your Father.

Immanuel, God with us, is your Savior's name.

Our Family

See what kind of love the Father has given to us, that we should be called children of God.

1 JOHN 3:1

Our true family is bigger than biology or legality. Our true family is the universal church. J.I. Packer puts it this way:

> The immediate message of adoption to our hearts is surely this: Do I as a Christian understand myself? Do I know my own real identity? My own real destiny? I am a child of God. God is Father, heaven is my home; every day is one day nearer. My Savior is my brother; every Christian is my brother too.[1]

We really aren't alone. We have the help of our God, and we have each other to help as well. You have everyone in your church community to help with your kiddos. I am not advocating that you allow random people in your church to talk to your kids about sex. But if trusted friends or leaders in your church can help your kids understand the biblical view of sex in a way that complements your parenting efforts, by all means give your kids permission to talk to them.

My daughter was recently struggling at school with some social and academic pressures. She opened up to a dear friend of mine, someone she considers a second mom of sorts, before she mentioned anything to me. I must admit, that stung a little. I wanted to be the one she would talk to first. But as I thought about it, I was filled with a gratefulness. To think I could meet every single one of my children's needs would be prideful and foolish. God has given us each other—this crazy family of broken sinners—to help each other. After I got over myself, I saw the value in having other adults in my kids' lives.

We have each other, and we should absolutely take advantage of that. Let your children know that it's okay to talk to someone besides you. I have come to see that as I loosen my grasp and exert less control over this part of my kids' lives, they are actually more apt to come to me.

My friend talked to my daughter and then encouraged her to talk to me as well. It ended up being a very sweet display of what our community should look like. Galatians 6:2 says, "Bear one another's burdens, and so fulfill the law of Christ." Surely some of our parenting tasks are included in those burdens we can share. When you speak into the lives of your friends' kids, and when other adults speak into the lives of your kids, you are fulfilling the law of Christ to love each other and care for one another.

Obviously, any adult you invite in must be utterly trustworthy. This is particularly important with sexual-oriented conversations. Also, you should always make sure the other adult will let you know anything you absolutely need to know. But remember, you don't need to know every single detail of their conversation. Trust God to use others in your child's life.

The Thorn in Your Flesh

Maybe your relationship with your teen is like Paul's thorn in the flesh.

> To keep me from becoming conceited because of the surpassing greatness of the revelations, a thorn was given me in the flesh, a messenger of Satan to harass me, to keep me from becoming conceited. Three times I pleaded with the Lord about this, that it should leave me. But he said to me, "My grace is sufficient for you, for my power is made perfect in weakness." Therefore I will boast all the more gladly of my weaknesses, so that the power of Christ may rest upon me. For the sake of Christ, then, I am content with weaknesses, insults, hardships, persecutions, and calamities. For when I am weak, then I am strong (2 Corinthians 12:7-10).

Now, I'm not saying our teens are messengers of Satan! And yet even as we love them, they are a constant source of pain in our lives. They are like a thorn in the flesh. We may even plead with the Lord to fix the relationship—to change their hearts or to change our hearts—but it seems as though we are stuck in a horrible pattern we cannot get out of.

Paul knows what that feels like. He pleaded with God to take away his thorn in the flesh, but God responded to Paul the way he responds to each of us: "My grace is sufficient. My power is made perfect in your weakness." Those two sentences are for you right now. If your relationship with your teen feels impossible, beyond repair, and without hope, hear your Father's words to you: "My grace is sufficient." He will help you. He will sustain you. He never leaves you. He isn't disappointed in your parenting.

Stop rehearsing and rehashing all the things you have done wrong and all the things you could have done differently. If you need to apologize to your child, ask for forgiveness, and seek reconciliation, do that. But please remember, you are hiding in the perfect work of Christ on your behalf. His grace is sufficient. It is enough. You don't need anything else.

This is a difficult truth to learn, but the joy that awaits is unmatched. You can know without any doubt at all that his grace is sufficient. It is never lacking. It will always be enough. He loves to show you his surpassing power and greatness in your weakest moments. So instead of remembering your failures, remember his success on your behalf—and rejoice!

Ultimately, our true help and hope is God alone. Feeling weak in our parenting is actually good for us because it reminds us and pushes us to trust in something outside of ourselves. He is so worthy of your complete trust. Be informed, be educated, figure out the best way to talk to your kids...but after it is all said and done, rest in the knowledge that your heavenly Father knows, sees, and cares.

> Feeling weak in our parenting is actually good for us because it reminds us and pushes us to trust in something outside of ourselves.

Words for Moms

Mothering can be heartbreaking. We carry the weight of our kids' salvation in a very deep way. We find our identity in how our kids turn out, and this is a problem. It always leads to heartbreak. So please just remember God. Remember his grace. Remember that he sees you. Ask for help from friends. Don't try to do this all by yourself. You can't.

You don't have to. You can take every regret, every failed attempt, every missed opportunity, every ignored opportunity and lay them at the feet of your Savior. He is your great high priest who sympathizes with you. He longs to comfort you. He is near to the brokenhearted. Whether you are brokenhearted by your own sin, by the sin of your children, or by both, he is near. Lean into him. Let him be your help and hope. If you have a spouse who is also a Christian, talk to them about your broken heart and ask them to pray with and for you. It is easy to look for someone or something to blame when things seem to be going wrong. Resist that temptation and just seek the Lord. Stay close to him. Rehearse the ways he has been faithful to you.

Please don't find your identity in the way your kids have turned out. Find your identity in Christ. It is the most important thing about you, and it will give you the courage to get up and try again tomorrow. There is hope and there is help in him.

Words for Dads

We dads typically don't like to deal in the category of weakness. We want to be seen as strong leaders, strong fathers, strong Christians. We don't want to be described as weak. God is so great though—he does his best work when we are weak. He doesn't need our strength to forgive or to save. You are not perfect, you are not able to be perfect, and thankfully, you are not expected to be perfect. Instead, you can be a picture of the grace of God to your teenagers. You can be a conduit for his grace to flow into their lives.

In this chapter we talked about the apostle Paul's thorn in the flesh, his messenger from Satan, and how God's strength was perfected in his weakness. Dad, it is okay to be weak. It is okay to not have everything under control. It is okay to help your teens by sharing your own brokenness. Dear brother, this is where your strength shines—your strength comes from the Lord, the one who provides you with help in the midst of crisis. The psalmist asks this great question: "From where does my help come?" (Psalm 121:1).

When you discover that your teen is looking at porn, when you learn that your teen is pregnant, you ask yourself, *How have I failed? What am I going to do? Where will I get the help I need to face the day?* The psalmist says, "My help comes from the LORD, who made heaven and earth" (verse 2). Look to Jesus, brother, the one who promises never to leave you or forsake you. Then lead your teen to Jesus in hope, in repentance, in forgiveness, and in obedience. Jesus is your strength and shield, an ever-present hope in times of distress and trouble. Psalm 28:7 says, "The LORD is my strength and my shield; in him my heart trusts, and I am helped; my heart exults, and with my song I give thanks to him."

TALKING POINTS

This is another topic that you can ask questions about. The questions below and from the previous chapter are going to be difficult to ask, but reassure your child that you are just there to listen and not to defend yourself. If you need to ask for forgiveness from your child, please take the time to do that. And if you do ask for forgiveness do not follow the "I am sorry for...but if you had just acted differently" model. Just own your own sin. Let them see that you believe the gospel. Let them see that you believe in the forgiveness of Christ.

- Ask your kids if they have felt a lot of pressure from you to perform or to look and act a certain way.

- Ask them if they feel that pressure more in front of certain people. The answer to this question will be very telling about the people in your life whose opinions matter the most.

10

Sex Is More Than a List of Dos and Don'ts
The Gospel and the Whole Self

As Moses lifted up the serpent in the wilderness, so must the Son of Man be lifted up, that whoever believes in him may have eternal life. For God so loved the world, that he gave his only Son, that whoever believes in him should not perish but have eternal life.

JOHN 3:14-16

The easiest thing in the world would be to sit down with my kids and a piece of poster board, a sharpie, and a ruler. First, I would listen to all their concerns about what we were about to do.

"Are you going to make us do a craft, Mom?"

"Mom, please don't make us do a craft. You are so bad at it."

"Mumsy (yes, that is what a couple of my kids call me), remember that time when we homeschooled and we sat you down and did an intervention, begging you not to try to attempt crafts?"

Next, I would attempt to draw a semi-straight line somewhere near the center of the poster board. (Somehow, when God was handing out the crafting genes, he skipped right over me.) On the top of one side I would write "Allowed," and on the top of the other side I would write

"Not Allowed." Under the "Not Allowed" side I would write all the sexual activities that my kids are not allowed to do. I would start with the big, obvious ones.

Rule number one: "No sex outside the covenant of marriage." Looking at each of my three kids, I would make sure they understood. "You all have that? No. Sex. Outside. The. Covenant. Of. Marriage. Okay, next rule."

I would attempt to go on to "No pornography," but then I would feel the need to clarify "No sex outside the covenant of marriage," so I would add a sub-point just to be safe. "No being alone in a bedroom with the door closed." Then I would realize that might not be far enough. Because, let's be honest, you can have sex in a bedroom with a door that is opened. So I would amend sub-point number one to say, "Actually, you can't be in a bedroom alone with someone of the opposite sex even if the door is open."

But then I would think of some other places that one might have sex other than a bedroom, so I would add sub-point number two: "Also, no being in a car alone with someone of the opposite sex." Finally, I would pause and think of even more places one can have sex, and then I would come up with the clearest rule of all—sub-point number three: "Never be alone with anyone of the opposite sex, anywhere, anytime."

My kids would look at each other with exasperation in their eyes and then look at me with the "Mom, you've finally gone crazy" look. (I am very familiar with that look.)

Now we would be ready to move on to rule number two: "Never look at pornography." I would immediately see the inadequacy of this rule because truth be told, there are plenty of things to look at that aren't exactly porn but that would make you want to look at porn. So to make sure my kids would never even want to look at porn, I would add sub-point one: "No Instagram accounts." (I hear those can be very dangerous and have inappropriate pictures.)

Sub-point number two would be, "No social media of any kind." But then I would remember the checkout line at the grocery store and the Victoria's Secret store at the mall with all the women showing lots of skin, and I would add sub-point number three: "No looking at men or women who are wearing anything that resembles undergarments." Then I would remember that we live in Southern California and that we pretty much can't go anywhere without seeing someone dressed like that, so I would add sub-point number four: "If there is a chance you might see someone wearing a small amount of clothing, walk with your eyes glued to the ground. Yes, even at the beach."

Before I could move on to rule number three, I would feel how exasperating it was going to be, so I would just say, "Let's focus on the other side of the chart. What *can* you do?" Under "Allowed" I would write in big letters, "Be sexually inactive in every single way."

I would put my Sharpie down firmly on the kitchen table and ask, "Any questions?" Before they could answer, I would say, "Good talk" and walk out of the room.

I'm sure you see how ridiculous this would be. (Or maybe you're thinking it's a pretty good idea.) The first problem with making a chart like this is that there are not enough rules to control human sexuality. Paul actually talks about this in Romans 7, as we will see shortly.

The second problem with the chart is that we end up becoming modern-day Pharisees. We would be expanding the commands of God more and more so we wouldn't break the original commands. Jesus talks about expanding or altering God's laws in Matthew 23. He has some very strong words for the Pharisees. We will look at those later in this chapter as well.

God's Dos and Don'ts

But first let's review the reason God gives us his law. First, as we saw in chapter 9, God gives us his law to show us our desperate need for a Savior. His holy law is given to us to crush our own self-confidence and to point us to something outside of ourselves to help.

Second, God gives us the law to make us grateful for Christ's perfect keeping of it in our place. When we see the commands against sexual immorality, we may be able to say, "I have never committed adultery." But can you say you have never even looked at someone lustfully? The answer to that is no. You can't say that. I can't say that...only one person could say that. Christ kept perfectly every law related to sexuality, and he did it for you and for me. As others have said, "He received the worst about me, and I received the best about him." When we look at God's holy and perfect law, we can then turn our gaze to Christ. He perfectly kept the law on our behalf so that before God, we stand righteous, wholly free from condemnation.

> He perfectly kept the law on our behalf so that before God, we stand righteous, wholly free from condemnation.

Third, the law is given to help us to see what gospel-engendered gratitude looks like. The law was not given to make us sexually pure. Rules can't make us clean. The law was given to show us we need something outside of us to give us a purity that is not of our own doing. That gift then moves us to gratefulness for what God has done for us. So when you are talking to your kids about your family rules, please make sure you understand that having all the right rules can't save your kids. Only Christ can.

Do Not Covet

Now let's look at what the apostle Paul has to say about rules and what they can and can't do.

> What then shall we say? That the law is sin? By no means! Yet if it had not been for the law, I would not have known sin. For I would not have known what it is to covet if the law had not said, "You shall not covet." But sin, seizing an opportunity through the commandment, produced in me all kinds of covetousness. For apart from the law, sin lies dead (Romans 7:7-8).

Matthew Henry explains these verses this way: "Ever since Adam ate forbidden fruit, we have all been fond of forbidden paths; the diseased appetite is carried out most strongly towards that which is hurtful and prohibited."[1] When we see the law, something wicked in our hearts is drawn to break it. The fact that something is prohibited makes us want it more. Let me explain.

When my (Jessica's) boys were about 11 and 13, we were on a hike and saw a sign that said, "No Hiking Past This Marker." Immediately both boys ran to the other side of the sign and asked me to take their picture. That is exactly how the law works in our lives. My boys wouldn't have thought of going to that side of the trail if they hadn't seen that sign.

Now, don't get me wrong—God's perfect and holy laws about sexual purity are good and are meant for our good. Nothing is wrong with his law, but everything is wrong with us. It is important to understand how the human heart works. The rules that we give our kids and the good commands in the Bible cannot save our children or change their hearts. If anything, those rules entice them. That was Paul's experience, that was my boys' experience, and that is my experience as well.

I am not advocating that we abolish all rules. I just want to encourage you to put your hope in something other than the rules. Our natural tendency is to put our trust in anything that we think will guarantee a certain outcome. We despise trusting God with open hands. Please make rules for your family, and make those rules clear to your children, but ultimately trust God. Trust that he has you. Trust that he knows what is best for you. Trust that he will never leave or forsake you even in the midst of difficult circumstances.

> I am not advocating that we abolish all rules. I just want to encourage you to put your hope in something other than the rules.

Building Fences, Adding Burdens

You leave the commandment of God and hold to the tradition of men.
MARK 7:8

The Pharisees were notorious for keeping God's law outwardly. They were known for their ceremonious and punctilious adherence to every single rule. They were so committed to keeping God's law that they made extra rules—sort of like fences around the original law—so they wouldn't even get close to breaking the moral code. They demanded that others follow these petty, unreasonable additions to the law.

The truly ironic thing is that they did this only with the laws they wanted to, and then they ignored many other portions of God's laws. Jesus took them to task for this very thing.

> He said to them, "Well did Isaiah prophesy of you hypocrites, as it is written, 'This people honors me with their lips, but their heart is far from me; in vain do they worship me, teaching as doctrines the commandments of men.' You leave the commandment of God and hold to the tradition of men." And he said to them, "You have a fine way of rejecting the commandment of God in order to establish your tradition! For Moses said, 'Honor your father and your mother'; and, 'Whoever reviles father or mother must surely die.' But you say, 'If a man tells his father or his mother, "Whatever you would have gained from me is Corban"' (that is, given to God)—then you no longer permit him to do anything for his father or mother, thus making void the word of God by your tradition that you have handed down. And many such things you do" (Mark 7:6-13).

This passage is a bit hard to understand, but the bottom line is this: The Pharisees changed God's law. They built an extra fence around it to serve their own purposes. *The Lutheran Study Bible* explains the passage in this way:

> He describes them as failing to obey the Fourth Commandment ("Honor your father and your mother") because they consider it more important to give special offerings than to support elderly parents. Such piety is ultimately self-serving and a sham.[2]

In Matthew, Jesus has more strong words about the scribes and the Pharisees.

> They preach, but do not practice. They tie up heavy burdens, hard to bear, and lay them on people's shoulders, but they themselves are not willing to move them with their finger. They do all their deeds to be seen by others (Matthew 23:2-5).

You may be wondering where I am going with all these verses about Pharisees making extra rules. I want to caution you from doing the same thing with your children. Sometimes when we give our children rules to protect them, we are actually laying heavy burdens on their shoulders. Again, if we are looking to rules to save our children, we will end up being too strict. Rules cannot change the human heart—that is solely up to the Holy Spirit.

The Pharisees aren't the only ones who dabbled in adding rules. It was part of the fall of man. God told Adam and Eve, "Don't eat of the fruit." Eve then told the serpent that God had said, "Don't touch or eat of the fruit." For some reason she made God's law to be more than it was. We do the same thing. Eve's extra rules did not keep her from breaking the original law from God, and our extra rules won't help us either. So before you establish rules for your family, be clear with your kids about what the *Bible* commands and what *you* are asking. Make the differentiation. It is an important one.

Are you throwing your arms up in frustration? *So now what? Are you saying I shouldn't make any rules and that rules don't help?*

Let me once again say that you should have family rules. Your kids should be very aware of your rules and, more importantly, what the Bible says about sexual ethics. Rules are important, and God's law is good and holy. So don't shy away from putting rules in place, but always remember the point of the rules. Always remember that even if your kids follow every single rule, they won't necessarily be pure before God. And you don't need to feel hopeless if your kids break the rules. The only people God redeems are lawbreakers, because those are the only people there are. And don't let fear control you as you do establish rules. If you let fear of what might happen, or fear of what others might think, or fear of what your kids might do control you, your rules will be extreme and harsh. Let wisdom and the Bible be your guides.

Deeper Than Rule Keeping

Sexual holiness is more than keeping a couple of rules. As we have seen, Jesus talks about this very thing in Matthew 5:27-30.

> You have heard that it was said, "You shall not commit adultery." But I say to you that everyone who looks at a woman with lustful intent has already committed adultery with her in his heart. If your right eye causes you to sin, tear it out and throw it away. For it is better that you lose one of your members than that your whole body be thrown into hell. And if your right hand causes you to sin, cut it off and throw it away. For it is better that you lose one of your members than that your whole body go into hell.

The Message paraphrase puts it a bit more bluntly.

> You know the next commandment pretty well, too: "Don't go to bed with another's spouse." But don't think you've preserved your virtue simply by staying out of bed. Your heart can be corrupted by lust even quicker than your body. Those leering looks you think nobody notices—they also corrupt. Let's not pretend this is easier than it really is. If you want to live a morally pure life, here's what you have to do: You have to blind your right eye the moment you catch it in a lustful leer. You have to choose to live one-eyed or else be dumped on a moral trash pile. And you have to chop off your right hand the moment you notice it raised threateningly. Better a bloody stump than your entire being discarded for good in the dump.

Jesus doesn't lessen the rules; he takes them straight to the heart, where he drives a stake into all our self-righteousness. I love the way

Eugene Peterson puts it: "Don't think you've preserved your virtue by simply staying out of bed." We can and should set up rules for our kids, but even if they follow every single rule, that doesn't make them right with God. Jesus tells us it's about more than the rules—it's about our hearts.

Have you ever once looked at another person with lust in your heart? You are guilty of breaking the whole law. Let me share a definition of lust so that there is absolutely no confusion about this. Merriam-Webster defines lust as "a strong feeling of sexual desire." No wiggle room at all. We are all guilty. Every single one of us. And brother or sister, that's the point. That's why Jesus takes it further than just an outward action and applies it to inward thoughts. He wants us to see just how desperately we need him. How singularly helpless we are without someone from the outside crashing into our lives to save us.

> How singularly helpless we are without someone from the outside crashing into our lives to save us.

In one sense, he makes the rules impossible, and even though that might seem overly harsh, it is actually the best thing for us. Because when we are at the end of ourselves, that's when we find that the answer was never in ourselves to begin with. This goes for our kids too. They need his gloriously devastating news. We need Jesus. We are completely lost without him.

Jesus offers us an option. If you want to do this whole sexually pure thing on your own, if you want to make sure you never look at someone with strong sexual desire, go ahead and just pop your eye out. That's how far you will have to go if you are going to rely on your own righteousness. If you want to make sure you never touch anyone inappropriately, go ahead and cut that arm off. You may be blind and maimed, but at least you have a better chance of getting into heaven on your own merit. Sounds a bit ridiculous, right? So is the thought that we can remain completely sexually pure on our own.

A Changed Heart

We love because he first loved us.

1 JOHN 4:19

It is much easier to trust in a rock-solid list of rules than it is to trust the Holy Spirit to change, woo, and draw our kids' hearts. But the truth is, only God can change our kids' hearts. Our job is show them the glory of the gospel. We can build in them a robust theology of Christ's love for sinners.

A couple chapters ago, Joel touched on Thomas Chalmers's landmark sermon, "The Expulsive Power of a New Affection." In that piece he says this:

> We know of no other way by which to keep the love of the world out of our heart, than to keep in our hearts the love of God—and no other way by which to keep our hearts in the love of God, than building ourselves upon our most holy faith. That denial of the world which is not possible to him that dissents from the Gospel testimony, is possible even as all things are possible, to him that believeth. To try this without faith, is to work without the right tool or the right instrument. But faith worketh by love; and the way of expelling from the heart the love which transgresseth the law, is to admit into its receptacles the love which fulfilleth the law.[3]

In more modern terms, just telling your kids that sexual misconduct is wrong or that they shouldn't love sexual misconduct is going to do absolutely nothing to change their hearts. Instead, build in them the truth that they are loved. Fan the flame of love for God. That is the only thing strong enough to curb our appetites.

You and I both know how strong sexual desires are, and we need something even stronger to control us. Knowing the right thing to do doesn't stop us from doing the wrong thing. The only way to change our appetites or our desires is to totally and completely fall in love with Jesus and be totally and completely awestruck by his love for us.

We cannot reduce sexual purity to a checklist. It is much more complicated than that. Sexual desire is a good thing, a healthy thing, and part of how God created us, but it must be held in its proper place. Any desire that is elevated above our desire for God is an idol. By the work of the Holy Spirit, love for God and obsession with God's love for us are the only things that keep desires in check.

And the crazy cool part is that even if our desires or our kids' desires are not held in check, our God forgives every single sin. He forgives not only the respectable sins but even the dirtiest sins, the most shameful ones. That truth, the truth of his unrelenting forgiveness, is what will keep us coming back to him instead of hiding in shame. The beauty of his love for sinners, even sexual sinners, is what keeps our hearts in check.

First John 4:19 says, "We love because he first loved us." And that is the key. We love because he loved. When our hearts are so overwhelmed by the love of God for us, we won't have room for other loves. This great love is what we should be cultivating in our kids' lives. If our children are not saved or do not love God, we can share with them the good news that "at the right time Christ died for the ungodly" (Romans 5:6). Christ came for those who hated him.

How do we make it about more than the rules? We give the gospel too. We give the unrelenting love and boundless grace that is displayed in the life, death, and resurrection of Christ. So again, yes, yes, yes, give rules. Make them plain. But always, always, always, give the gospel too. Because even though your kids might be following your rules outwardly, our goal is a heart change. We want to dazzle our kids with the love of Christ.[4] Liz Edrington, who is part of Rooted ministries, puts it this way, "Love is so much more powerful than fear, and way too often fear becomes the prime motivator for saving sex until marriage."[5]

"Love is so much more powerful than fear,
and way too often fear becomes the prime
motivator for saving sex until marriage."

We must come at this from a different way than maybe we were taught or the way our churches sometimes teach now. We must let love motivate our kids' actions instead of using fear to control them. If your child is not a Christian or doesn't profess love for God, you will have to try to use the rules to help guide their behavior, but continue to hold the gospel out for them. Continue to show them the goodness and patience of our loving heavenly Father. Continue to call them home to the Father.

Ultimately, we need to understand that it is not our work to change hearts. So even if you do give your kids the gospel, the Holy Spirit has to do his work. So pray. Pray that God enlivens their hearts to the truth and goodness of his love. Pray that he uses you as the means to do that. And then rest. Don't put trust in anything you do, whether it's making the right rules or delivering the right gospel. Trust in him.

This thought should drive you to your knees in prayer. That's an uncomfortable position to be in, but when we rely on God's grace and beg for his help, we will find that the Holy Spirit is actually really good at his job. This may mean that he convicts your teens of sexual sin and they live changed lives. It may mean that he reassures your teen of forgiveness in Christ when they fail, and even though they fail over and over, they keep running back to their Savior. It may mean that he gives you grace and kindness and wisdom for rebellious and hard teens. Either way, God himself promises that he will never leave or forsake you. That's a pretty good promise to ground your entire set of rules in. Parent, you are loved. Remind your teens that they are too, and let God do his work.

Words for Moms

The only way you will be able to talk to your kids about the great love of Jesus in a contagious way is to be taken by his love for you. Find ways to stoke the fire of your heart with the gospel. Read books that talk about what God has done for you, not just about what you should be doing for him. Listen to any style of music you love and find him in the lyrics. Spend time talking to him. Spend time looking in the

Scriptures for examples of how he loves you. Surround yourself with friends who will remind you of the good news. Listen to preaching or podcasts that will move your heart toward him. Fall in love with the one who has loved you eternally.

Be purposeful when you talk to your kids about the rules. Make them plain, but as much as you can, avoid making the rules the point. The point is always Jesus. If your kids think your rules are unnecessarily harsh, be willing to hear them. Don't always assume you are right. Keep an attitude of humility—yes, even with your kids. And if your kids are hell-bent on not following the rules, pray for them. Take them to Jesus. You may have to take some drastic measures with them. Your relationship with them may be broken for a while. Do what you think God is calling you to do and then trust him. His grace is sufficient.

> Be purposeful when you talk to your kids about the rules. Make them plain, but as much as you can, avoid making the rules the point. The point is always Jesus.

Words for Dads

When you begin to consider how to engage your teens' hearts so they are motivated to live in a way that honors God, you must start with the gospel. The way we live has to do with more than just being given a list and being told to follow it. This isn't like work, where you have a task list to follow. Sex isn't like programming a computer, designing a user interface, or building a house. Those endeavors include steps you can take to produce the product you want regardless of whether your heart is right with God. Sex involves so much more—emotions, hormones, love, physical urges, and an understanding of what sex is meant to be. It's pretty clear why a list of dos and don'ts is inadequate, isn't it?

To help your teens understand how to deal with these intangible and sometimes insatiable urges, you have to equip them to meet those urges with the gospel. To help your teens deal with the guilt of sinning sexually, you have to meet their guilt with the gospel. And to do this,

Dad, you must understand the gospel. Your heart must be filled with the beauty and the wonder of what Christ has done for you.

Engage them with the glory of Christ and then set the rules in the context of a proper response to the God who loves them deeply. Set biblical rules for their sexual conduct, encourage them to offer their bodies as living sacrifices (Romans 12:1), but don't forget everything that comes before that in the book of Romans—the gospel!

This takes time. Being a father who is present takes time and effort. You may have to reprioritize your time in order to be with your teen. After a long day at work, you may have to take your teen out to dinner to talk with them. (You should be doing this anyway.) You must approach them in humility. Remember that you are a sinner saved by grace. Your heavenly Father loves you so much that he was willing to send the divine Word, Jesus, so that you would understand the gospel and live in light of it.

TALKING POINTS

We are almost to the end of our journey together. If you have talked about sex in a way that isn't biblical, or if you have tried to use manipulation or scare tactics to stop your kids from having sex, now would be the time to talk to them about grace.

- Talk to your children about how beautiful Jesus is. If there is a story of forgiveness that you can share with them from your past, please do that.

- Make your list of dos and don'ts very plain to your children, but assure them that the only way to be right before God is to trust in Jesus.

- Remind them again that they are loved no matter what. Make sure they hear this from you often.

A Super-Sexy Conclusion

We have covered a lot of ground since we first started. Honestly, for a brother and sister to be spending all this time writing a book about sex has been strange and at times hilarious. But this process has reminded us that we learn best in community. Processing information about topics that are uncomfortable works best in light of God's revelation and the community of believers.

If that is true for adults, how much more so for our kids? It is scary to approach our teens about a topic like this that could be so awkward, that might be painful for us, or that we would love to just go away. We have been careful to not give you everything to say, but instead to build for you a biblical way of thinking about this topic that takes into account the whole witness of Scripture in the light of Christ. This is key to every part of our lives.

The Bible isn't a script for all our conversations; it is a story that points us to Jesus. This is how we talk to our kids. When we tell them the story, we point them to Jesus. When we live their story with them, we point them to Jesus. When the two of us talk to parents, they often want to know the super-secret code words to fix their kids. There simply aren't any, and that's good. It keeps us relying on the Holy Spirit. It keeps us desperate for Jesus to work in our lives and in theirs.

The Bible isn't a script for all our conversations;
it is a story that points us to Jesus.

We hope you have seen that this is not about a one-time birds-and-bees conversation that is awkward and hurried and never brought up again. This is about multiple conversations over a lifetime. The truths of Scripture are about all of life, and Scripture doesn't record just one conversation, especially about sex! God knows that this is an important part of our lives that can include a lot of good and a lot of brokenness, so he tells us about it in historical accounts, wisdom literature, song, and direct instruction. God understands that we are multifaceted people who learn in different ways and have different life experiences, so he tells us the truth in different ways to help us understand his truth.

This is instructive for how we talk to our kids. We need to learn about our kids. Study them. Discover the way they learn. Find the best way to communicate with them. And then share the glorious truths of the gospel and sex with them in a way they will best understand.

We parents are given a great opportunity to walk through a full and rich life with our teens, helping them to understand how the glory of Christ is displayed, even in an area like sex. If we are to do this well, the gospel, the good news of salvation, must be the air we breathe at home. We get to tell our kids over and over again that life is not easy, that sex is not easy, that life is sometimes incredibly broken, and that sex sometimes is too. But sex can be one of life's most beautiful gifts. Our good God is bringing restoration through his Son, and that restoration starts even now. We all give in to temptation and fall into sin, but Jesus frees us from sin's guilt and power, and the Holy Spirit works in our lives every single day.

We parents are given a great opportunity to walk through a
full and rich life with our teens, helping them to understand
how the glory of Christ is displayed, even in an area like sex.

Teach your children that their bodies aren't something bad to be contained until marriage and then let loose. Teach them the loveliness and complexity of sexuality. It is hard work, but we have the Holy Spirit to help and to guide and to clean up our messes. One thing I (Jessica) always pray when I am done talking with my kids about something serious is that God would help them to forget the dumb, unhelpful, or unbiblical stuff that I probably said and that he would instead make alive all the things that pointed them to him.

We have avoided getting into the nitty gritty details concerning every sexual act. We didn't want to give you a list to follow; instead, we wanted to help you start building a lifestyle. If this disappointed you, we are sorry. But we can share with you a list of books to help you on your journey to living a life of understanding. The books listed at the end of this conclusion are helpful, well researched, and well written. We don't agree with everything that is written in all of them, but they helped us understand different sides of the arguments.

Thank you for taking this journey with us. Our hope and prayer is that God will use this book not only in your family but in generations to come. We have prayed that as you are able to open up to your children about sex, you will find yourself able to talk to them about everything. We hope you heard good news throughout the book and that you can share that good news with your kids.

Create an atmosphere of grace in your house. Remind them of who they are in Christ. Share with them the beauty of forgiven sins. Talk to them about the craziness of justification. Give them something to smile about. Mom or Dad, in order to do those things, you are going to have to be reminding yourself of the same things. So as a way of helping you do that, we want to close with Psalm 103. Please don't skip over or skim this. Let the Word of the Lord bring life to you and your family.

> Bless the LORD, O my soul,
> and all that is within me,
> bless his holy name!
> Bless the LORD, O my soul,
> and forget not all his benefits,

who forgives all your iniquity,
who heals all your diseases,
who redeems your life from the pit,
who crowns you with steadfast love and mercy,
who satisfies you with good
so that your youth is renewed like the eagle's.

The LORD works righteousness
and justice for all who are oppressed.
He made known his ways to Moses,
his acts to the people of Israel.
The LORD is merciful and gracious,
slow to anger and abounding in steadfast love.
He will not always chide,
nor will he keep his anger forever.
He does not deal with us according to our sins,
nor repay us according to our iniquities.
For as high as the heavens are above the earth,
so great is his steadfast love toward those who fear him;
as far as the east is from the west,
so far does he remove our transgressions from us.
As a father shows compassion to his children,
so the LORD shows compassion to those who fear him.
For he knows our frame;
he remembers that we are dust.

As for man, his days are like grass;
he flourishes like a flower of the field;
for the wind passes over it, and it is gone,
and its place knows it no more.
But the steadfast love of the LORD is from everlasting to
everlasting on those who fear him, and his righteousness
to children's children,
to those who keep his covenant
and remember to do his commandments.
The LORD has established his throne in the heavens,
and his kingdom rules over all.

We confess that we lied about this chapter title—this is the most unsexy conclusion ever written. But God uses the ordinary means of everyday, awkward conversations to show us how incredibly strong he is when he magnifies his own name. Rest and trust in him.

REFERENCE LIST

Books About Chastity

Lauren Winner, *Real Sex: The Truth About Chastity* (Brazos Press, 2006).

Books About Sex

Peter Jones, *God of Sex: How Spirituality Defines Your Sexuality* (Main Entry Editions, 2014).

Andreas Kostenberger, *God, Marriage, and Family: Rebuilding the Biblical Foundation* (Crossway, 2010).

Jenell Williams Paris, *The End of Sexual Identity: Why Sex Is Too Important to Define Who We Are* (IVP Books, 2011).

John Piper and Justin Taylor, *Sex and the Supremacy of Christ* (Crossway, 2005).

Joseph W. Smith III, *Sex and Violence in the Bible: A Survey of Explicit Content in the Holy Book* (P&R Publishing, 2014).

Books About Social Media

Danah Boyd, *It's Complicated: The Social Lives of Networked Teens* (Yale University Press, 2015).

Kristen Hatton, *Face Time: Your Identity in a Selfie World* (New Growth Press, 2017).

Books About Homosexuality

Sam Allberry, *Is God Anti-Gay? And Other Questions About Homosexuality, the Bible and Same-Sex Attraction* (The Good Book Company, 2013).

Rosaria Champagne Butterfield, *The Secret Thoughts of an Unlikely Convert: An English Professor's Journey into Christian Faith* (Crown & Covenant, 2012).

Stanley N. Gundry and Preston Sprinkle, eds., *Two Views on Homosexuality, the Bible, and the Church* (Zondervan, 2016).

Wesley Hill, *Washed and Waiting: Reflections on Christian Faithfulness and Homosexuality* (Zondervan, 2016).

Preston Sprinkle, *People to Be Loved: Why Homosexuality Is Not Just an Issue* (Zondervan, 2015).

Books About Sexual Abuse

Justin and Lindsey Holcomb, *Rid of My Disgrace: Hope and Healing for Victims of Sexual Assault* (Crossway, 2011).

Notes

Why We Need the Bible's Story About Sex

1. Stanley J. Grenz, *Sexual Ethics: An Evangelical Perspective* (Louisville, KY: Westminster John Knox, 1997), 24.

2. Robert A. J. Gagnon, "Sexuality," in *Dictionary for Theological Interpretation of the Bible*, ed. Kevin J. Vanhoozer (Grand Rapids: Baker, 2005), 739.

3. Grenz, *Sexual Ethics*, 82.

Chapter 1: The Creation of Sex and Identity

1. Leah McGrath Goodman, "Fifty Shades of Amish: A Strange Genre of the Romance Novel," *Newsweek*, April 26, 2015, http://www.newsweek.com/2015/05/08/fifty-shades-amish-strange-genre -romance-novel-324940.html.

2. Anugrah Kumar, "Are Most Single Christians in America Having Sex?" *Christian Post*, September 28, 2011, http://www.christianpost.com/news/are-most-single-christians-in-america-having -sex-56680/.

3. Dan Allender, *God Loves Sex* (Grand Rapids, MI: Baker Publishing Group, October 28, 2014), 245.

4. Allender, *God Loves Sex*, 1.

5. Jenell Williams Paris, *The End of Sexual Identity: Why Sex Is Too Important to Define Who We Are* (Downers Grove, IL: InterVarsity Press, February 28, 2011), 13.

6. Justin and Lindsey Holcomb, *Rid of My Disgrace: Hope and Healing for Victims of Sexual Abuse* (Wheaton, IL: Crossway, 2011), 163.

7. When we say that one member of the Trinity sent the other we should not imagine that the sent member goes begrudgingly. It is not like when I send my child to bed and they go angrily or sadly; it is the will, joy, and desire of the sent member to go in order to bring pleasure to the sending member. This is very important to remember as it helps us to understand the self-giving nature of love and the self-giving nature of our sexuality.

8. See, for example, Macrina Cooper-White, "Watching Porn Linked to Less Gray Matter in the Brain," *Huffpost*, June 2, 2014, http://www.huffingtonpost.com/2014/06/02/porn-less-gray-matter -brain_n_5418607.html; Stephanie Pappas, "Porn May 'Shut Down' Part of Your Brain," *Live Science*, April 18, 2012, https://www.livescience.com/19755-porn-shut-visual-brain.html.

Chapter 2: Stories of Sexual Brokenness and God's Redemption

1. Martin Luther King Jr., *Strength to Love* (Minneapolis, MN: Fortress Press, 2010), 47.

2. See Ken Sande, "Four Promises of Forgiveness," *Peacemaker Ministries,* September 22, 2014, http://peacemaker.net/project/four-promises-of-forgiveness/.

3. Madlen Davies, "Revealed...how watching porn really affects your BRAIN," *Daily Mail,* August 14, 2015, http://www.dailymail.co.uk/health/article-3196809/It-induces-addiction-makes-men-hopeless-bed-discover-porn-affect-BRAIN.html; Tia Ghose, "5 ways porn affects the brain," *Fox News Health,* October 14, 2015, http://www.foxnews.com/health/2015/10/14/5-ways-porn-affects-brain.html.

Chapter 3: The Wisdom of Sexual Fidelity

1. This idea is drawn from a talk given by Zach Eswine as well as his commentary on Ecclesiastes. Zach Eswine, "Finding Rest When There Isn't Any, Part 1," from the Imperfect Pastor Ministry Weekend 2017, https://ibcd.org/finding-rest-when-there-isnt-any-part-1; Zach Eswine, *Recovering Eden: The Gospel According to Ecclesiastes* (Phillipsburg, New Jersey: P&R Publications, 2014), 3-10.

2. As an aside, this is helpful to us in our modern world as we think about talking to our teens about sex. We should appeal to things they understand and interact with daily to help us in making the case for biblical sexuality. Also, talking about sexuality is not just for moms, as this passage of Scripture demonstrates. A dad's role in this discussion is vital.

3. The temptress could also be a tempter. I don't think this is meant for us to think that only women are at fault in the act of temptation. To blame only women denigrates women and lets men off the hook. This is unfair and goes against Jesus's teaching in Matthew 5:27-30 concerning lust and adultery.

4. This is anecdotal and I don't have any proof except for my own ears. I have heard this passage also used to say that loud women, women who are affectionate publicly, who are strong are harlots. This is also a grave misuse of this passage. The point of this passage is not the outward character of the woman but the inward desires of both of their hearts.

5. Iain M. Duguid, *The Song of Songs* (Wheaton, IL: Tyndale, 2015), 37-38. For a fuller understanding of the different ways the Song is interpreted, see Duguid's excellent summary, pages 24-38.

6. Lauren F. Winner, *Real Sex* (Grand Rapids, MI: Brazos Press, 2005), 41-42.

Chapter 4: Sex and the Consummation of the Kingdom of God

1. Sam Allberry, "How Celibacy Can Fulfill Your Sexuality," *The Gospel Coalition,* August 26, 2016, https://www.thegospelcoalition.org/article/how-celibacy-can-fulfill-your-sexuality.

2. Allberry.

3. C.S. Lewis, *Mere Christianity* (New York, NY: HarperCollins, 2001), 136-37.

4. See also Jeremiah 2:2; 31:32; Ezekiel 16:8-14,59-60; Hosea 2:7.

5. Thomas Chalmers, "The Expulsive Power of a New Affection," *Monergism,* https://www.monergism.com/thethreshold/sdg/Chalmers,%20Thomas%20-%20The%20Exlpulsive%20Power%20of%20a%20New%20Af.pdf.

6. For more on this, see Elyse Fitzpatrick, *Idols of the Heart* (Phillipsburg, NJ: P&R Publishing, 2002) and Tim Keller, *Counterfeit Gods* (London, UK: Penguin Books, 2011).

Chapter 5: Friend Goals

1. Paul Tripp, "Blindness to God's Process," *Wednesday's Word* (blog), July 3, 2013, https://www.paul tripp.com/wednesdays-word/posts/blindness-to-gods-process.

Chapter 6: Likes and Comments

1. Ira Glass, "Status Update," November 27, 2015, in *This American Life* (podcast), https://www .thisamericanlife.org/radio-archives/episode/573/status-update?act=0#play.

2. Amit Chowdhry, "Research Links Heavy Facebook and Social Media Usage to Depression," *Forbes*, April 30, 2016, https://www.forbes.com/sites/amitchowdhry/2016/04/30/study-links -heavy-facebook-and-social-media-usage-to-depression/; Megan Bennett, "Social media linked to student anxiety," *Columbia Chronicle*, May 12, 2014, http://www.columbiachronicle .com/health_and_tech/article_aa2daa9a-d7e4-11e3-9286-001a4bcf6878.html; Sharon Noguchi, "Teen health: Depression, anxiety and social phobias rising in kids, educators say," *Mercury News*, August 12, 2016, http://www.mercurynews.com/2014/02/05/teen-health-depression -anxiety-and-social-phobias-rising-in-kids-educators-say/.

3. George Whitefield, *Selected Sermons of George Whitefield* (Oak Harbor, WA: Logos Research Systems, 1999).

4. There is a common misconception that Jesus never talks about hell, but he does. See Matthew 5:22,29-30; 10:28; 16:18; 23:15; Mark 9:43,45,47; Luke 12:5. This is not meant to be used as a fear tactic, but as a reality check. All sin deserves hell. Praise God for Jesus!

Chapter 7: Over-Sexualization

1. Josh Kramer, "The Hidden Message in the Architecture of *Steven Universe*," *Atlantic*, July 12, 2017, https://www.theatlantic.com/entertainment/archive/2017/07/the-peculiarly-magical-architect ure-of-steven-universe/533202/.

2. *Wonder Woman*, directed by Patty Jenkins, screenplay by Allan Heinberg, Burbank, CA: Warner Bros. Pictures, 2017.

3. Nancy Jo Sales, *American Girls: Social Media and the Secret Lives of Teenagers* (New York, NY: Vintage Books, 2017), 48.

4. Lisa Bennetts, "The Growing Demand for Prostitution," *Newsweek*, July 18, 2011, http://www .newsweek.com/growing-demand-prostitution-68493.

5. See, for example, "What Is Sex Trafficking?" *Shared Hope International*, https://sharedhope.org/ the-problem/what-is-sex-trafficking/; "The Connections Between Pornography and Sex Trafficking," *Covenant Eyes*, http://www.covenanteyes.com/2011/09/07/the-connections-between -pornography-and-sex-trafficking/#_edn10. The bibliography on this site is especially helpful.

6. Olivia Goldhill, "Why teenagers' obsession with porn is creating a generation of 20-year-old virgins," *Telegraph*, August 20, 2014, http://www.telegraph.co.uk/women/sex/11045859/Why-teenagers -obsession-with-porn-is-creating-a-generation-of-20-year-old-virgins.html.

7. Thomas Chalmers, "The Expulsive Power of a New Affection," *Monergism*, https://www.monergism .com/thethreshold/sdg/Chalmers,%20Thomas%20-%20The%20Exlpulsive%20Power%20 of%20a%20New%20Af.pdf.

8. John A. Younts, *Everyday Talk About Sex and Marriage* (Wapwallopen, PA: Shepherds Press, 2017), p. 38.

9. Visit *Undone Redone* (www.undoneredone.com) and *Covenant Eyes* (www.covenanteyes.com). Find a local counseling center at *Christian Counseling & Educational Foundation* (www.ccef.org).

Chapter 8: Soul Building Instead of Soul Crushing

1. This is the first occurrence of the two great commands. In this instance we only see the first of the two great commands. It gives us some insight as to how to respond to God when presented with his glory and majesty—with love.

2. Westminster Confession of Faith, chapter 18, section 4.

3. See John Calvin, *Institutes of the Christian Religion*, Book II (Philadelphia, PA: Westminster Press, 1960), 1.304-10.

Chapter 9: Help and Hope for Parents

1. J.I. Packer, *Knowing God* (Great Britain: InterVarsity Press, 1973), 258.

Chapter 10: Sex Is More Than a List of Dos and Don'ts

1. Matthew Henry, *Commentary on the Whole Bible, vol. 6 (Acts to Revelation)*, notes on Romans 7:7-14.

2. *The Lutheran Study Bible: English Standard Version* (St. Louis, MO: Concordia, 2009), 1667.

3. Thomas Chalmers, "The Expulsive Power of a New Affection," *Monergism*, https://www.monergism .com/thethreshold/sdg/Chalmers,%20Thomas%20-%20The%20Exlpulsive%20Power%20 of%20a%20New%20Af.pdf.

4. See Elyse Fitzpatrick and Jessica Thompson, *Give Them Grace: Dazzling Your Kids with the Love of Christ* (Wheaton, IL: Crossway, 2011).

5. Liz Edrington, "Practical Considerations for Teaching Students about Sex" (blog post), *Rooted*, March 24, 2015, https://www.rootedministry.com/blog/practical-considerations-for-teaching -students-about-sex/.